QUICK PREP COOKING
with Your INSTANT POT®

QUICK PREP COOKING
with Your INSTANT POT®

75 BIG-FLAVOR DISHES THAT REQUIRE MINIMAL WORK

Stefanie Bundalo

creator of Sarcastic Cooking

PAGE STREET
PUBLISHING CO.

PAGE STREET
PUBLISHING CO.

To my boys:
MIKE, ANDY, JACK AND WEEZER

TABLE *of* CONTENTS

INTRODUCTION

Oh, good! You picked this book up off the shelf, which means you're an Instant Pot® lover, a novice or you just got one as a gift and have no idea what to do with it. You're in luck, because I've traversed and conquered all three of those phases. In this book, I will answer your multi-cooker questions, calm your fears about a device that shoots out hot steam and give you a bunch of delicious new ideas for your beloved multi-cooker.

Whether you are team Instant Pot or Crock-Pot® Express Crock, this thing can get the job done! Every recipe in this book passed a fifteen-minute, hands-on prep test. They were all made using the Instant Pot Duo and the Crock-Pot Express Crock 6-quart (6-L) multi-cookers. All recipes endured the rigorous examination of some people with a lot of opinions when it comes to good food. I wanted these people to see the end result and say, "This really came from an Instant Pot?"

But first, because we both know what brought you here, let me tell you what brought me here.

I began tinkering with my blog, Sarcastic Cooking, back in 2011. I was foolishly trying to turn a lifelong passion and hobby into a career. I was new to the blog scene and a bit naïve. I sometimes made overly complex recipes and served them up on the site with poor lighting and a novel to boot, as you did in the dark ages of blogging. But never before had I felt like I'd finally found the thing that I was meant to be doing in life. It was great to just keep cooking all day long and to share my food with all my imaginary Internet friends. I remember feeling proud and overwhelmed all at once, all the time.

Long before that, though, this journey with food began back in the kitchen of my parents' house. For my two younger brothers and me, food was always fun. We would make each other drink cups full of crazy mixtures such as toothpaste and hot sauce in between learning how to make the best grilled cheese sandwiches and scrambled eggs. (Fear not; there are no dishes with toothpaste and hot sauce in this book.)

We were rarely picky and pretty much enjoyed everything my mom threw at us. Well, until my stint as a vegetarian from 1999 to 2006. Then I had to start cooking more and get a little crafty with my food. If you didn't want what Mom was cooking, you were on your own!

After college, I worked for a while as a restaurant inspector. It was fascinating, and I found myself more concerned with the recipes these joints were making as opposed to enforcing an out-of-date countertop surface violation. When airing my job grievances to a good friend of mine, she suggested I start a food blog.

So here we are today, and that blog has since evolved along with my cooking skills—even though the pride and overwhelmed feeling still remain. I love cooking and always feel like I can be doing more in the kitchen. I have evolved too. I am now about to very cautiously step over the edge into my (gulp) mid-30s, and I've published my writing and recipes in a book. Gah, pinch me!

I also now have two kids under the age of five at home with me most of the time and a husband who comes home at three o'clock with the phrase "What's for dinner?" on his tongue instead of "Hello, dear, how was your day?"

The time for complicated cooking has come and gone, just like my 20s. Kiss it goodbye! In this day and age, given the pressures of everyday life, it feels like a blessing to weasel out twenty minutes for a meal. Lucky for you, with this book, all I am asking for is fifteen minutes or less. That is all you need to make a fun, tasty and easy meal. You can do anything for fifteen minutes a day if you really set your mind to it, right?

Just because a meal is quick doesn't mean it has to lack flavor or originality. I like to keep my food fun so I don't get bored. If you never tire of these meals and can stun your friends and family when you tell them they came from an Instant Pot, then my job and the mission of this cookbook are complete.

I understand how crucial mealtime is in your house. It can feel hectic, but it is supposed to be a time to nourish your body and recharge after a long day or long week. This book is basically my commitment to take care of you. I will make sure that your meals satisfy and give you comfort.

With this book, we'll cook up some good food, have fun and share a few laughs along the way.

Stefanie Bundalo

FUSS-FREE MEATS & MAINS

When I got married, I put my slow cooker to good use, cooking for two with all the time in the world, leaving all the pots and pans for my husband to clean up. We operate under the rule "if you cook, you don't clean up." (It works—implement it immediately!) A few years into marriage, all the time and prep work slow cooker meals required started to bog me down. The last thing I wanted to see in a recipe's instructions was "brown before placing in the slow cooker." Especially when busy nights meant dirty dishes either had to be left until the next day or, gasp, washed using my own two hands.

Now, we have the Instant Pot! Every step is done in one pot. Only one dish to wash? Sign me up to be the dinner hero who cooks AND cleans up afterward!

If you're able to carve out fifteen minutes in your day for some quick prep, using the Instant Pot's many functions is a dream for meats and mains. Who wouldn't love walking in the door to Sped-Up Classic Chipotle Carnitas Tacos (page 56) or My Reuben Semi-Sliders (page 51)? On days when you don't feel like spending a lot of time cooking, it is great to be able to sauté and pressure cook an otherwise time-consuming meal in a snap. The Blackened Whole Faux-sted Chicken (page 48) cooks in less than an hour!

Just because you lost your sanity somewhere throughout the day doesn't mean you should have to lose out on a good dinner too.

PEACH & TOMATO BRUSCHETTA
Chicken

PREP TIME: 10 MINUTES
COOK TIME: 20 MINUTES OR 6 HOURS
SERVES 4

I like peaches on their own. But I love them more in savory dishes. Peaches in the summertime with some fresh tomatoes and a crusty piece of bread is my jam! Peaches add a level of sweetness and brighten up something as simple as a chicken breast. I would even suggest saving a little of the pretty peach-and-tomato mixture for topping the chicken when it is done cooking.

1½ lbs (680 g) boneless, skinless chicken breasts (3–4 breasts)

½ tsp salt, plus more to taste

¼ tsp freshly ground black pepper, plus more to taste

1 clove garlic, grated

1 tbsp (15 ml) extra-virgin olive oil

2 tbsp (30 ml) lemon juice

1 tsp balsamic vinegar

⅓ cup (50 g) diced red onion

1 peach, pitted and diced

¾ cup (135 g) diced tomatoes

Fresh basil, for garnish

Season each side of the chicken breasts with salt, pepper and the garlic. Rub the garlic into the chicken breasts.

Add the olive oil to the Instant Pot. Press "Sauté." Wait 1 minute for the pot to heat. Add the chicken breasts and sear for 5 minutes on each side.

While the chicken cooks, mix together the lemon juice, vinegar, onion, peach and tomatoes. Reserve 1 to 2 tablespoons (12 to 24 g) for garnish after the chicken is cooked through.

After 10 minutes of searing the chicken, press "Cancel." Flip the chicken breasts. Top with the peach-and-tomato mixture.

Secure the lid with the steam vent in the closed position. Press "Pressure Cook" until the display light is underneath "High Pressure." Use the "–/+" button to adjust the time to read 20 minutes.

When the timer is done, quick release the pressure. Transfer the chicken to a serving platter. Top with the remaining peach–tomato bruschetta, fresh basil, a good pinch of salt and freshly cracked black pepper.

SLOW COOKER OPTION: After searing the chicken on each side, add the lemon juice, balsamic vinegar and onion to the Instant Pot. Close the lid with the vent open. Set to "Slow Cook" on low for 6 hours. Mix in the peach, tomato and basil at the end before serving.

NASHVILLE HOT CHICKEN *Tacos*

PREP TIME: 15 MINUTES
COOK TIME: 8 HOURS OR 30 MINUTES
SERVES 2-4

I loooove fried chicken. I also love avoiding hot splatters of frying oil. With this recipe, you get the best of both worlds. No frying and all that hot, spicy, Nashville–fried chicken flavor. The truly great part about this recipe is you can either pressure cook the chicken at the last minute or set it and forget it with the slow cooker setting if you have a real life to attend to. The results will be equally delicious.

½ cup (120 ml) low-sodium chicken stock

1 tbsp (8 g) cornstarch

2 tbsp (15 g) cayenne pepper

1 tbsp (8 g) brown sugar

1 tsp smoked paprika

½ tsp garlic powder

½ tsp salt

¼ tsp freshly ground black pepper

2 large boneless, skinless chicken breasts

8-10 flour tortillas

½ cup (75 g) diced dill pickle, optional

1 cup (50 g) shredded romaine lettuce

Pico de gallo, cilantro and crumbled queso fresco, for garnish

Add the stock and cornstarch to the Instant Pot. Whisk to combine. Add the cayenne pepper, brown sugar, paprika, garlic powder, salt and pepper. Whisk to combine.

Cut each chicken breast in half widthwise. Add to the Instant Pot.

If you're slow cooking the chicken, secure the lid and leave the vent in the open position. Press the "Slow Cook" button so the display light is under "Less." Press the "−/+" button until the time displays 8 hours.

If you're pressure cooking the chicken, secure the lid and close the vent. Press "Pressure Cook." Hit the "Pressure Level" button until the display light is under "High Pressure." Adjust the "−/+" button until the display reads 30 minutes. When the timer is done, quick release the pressure.

Shred the chicken using two forks. Add equal portions of meat to the tortillas. Top each taco with the pickle, lettuce, pico de gallo, cilantro and queso fresco.

TIP: If you are sensitive to very spicy things, reduce the amount of cayenne pepper to 1 tablespoon (8 g).

Cuban PICADILLO TACOS

PREP TIME: 10 MINUTES
COOK TIME: 6 HOURS
SERVES 4-6

I have never met a taco I didn't like. I am a devout follower of #TacoTuesday. I am always open to trying any kind of taco or even taco-fying something. When I started making these tacos, I knew they were something out of the ordinary. The combination of sweet, spicy, salty and slightly pickled flavors definitely packs a punch. Slow cooking the beef really brings all those flavors to the forefront. You won't want to put too many toppings on these tacos to take away from the star of the show: the meat!

1 lb (450 g) lean ground beef

7 oz (202 g) canned fire-roasted diced tomatoes, drained

1 jalapeño, seeded and diced

3 cloves garlic, grated

½ onion, diced

¼ cup (40 g) golden raisins

⅓ cup (50 g) Castelvetrano olives, pitted and sliced

1 tbsp (15 ml) red wine vinegar

¼ tsp cayenne pepper

½ tsp ground cumin

½ tsp salt, plus more to taste

¼ tsp black pepper, plus more to taste

⅛ tsp ground cinnamon

1 dried bay leaf

8-10 hard taco shells

1 cup (75 g) shredded lettuce

¾ cup (85 g) shredded Mexican-blend cheese

OPTIONAL TOPPINGS

Pico de gallo

Sliced radish

Fresh chopped cilantro

Sliced avocado

Add the ground beef to the Instant Pot. Use a wooden spoon or potato masher to break apart the beef.

Add the diced tomatoes, jalapeño, garlic, onion, raisins, olives, vinegar, cayenne, cumin, salt, pepper and cinnamon. Mix to combine.

Add the bay leaf. Secure the lid and leave the steam valve in the open venting position.

Press "Slow Cook" until the display light is underneath "Less." Press the "−/+" button until the time display reads 6 hours.

When the timer is done, remove the lid and mix the meat. Use a wooden spoon to break apart any big pieces of beef. Add more salt and pepper to taste.

Spoon the mixture into the taco shells. Top with shredded lettuce and shredded cheese. Use any additional toppings you desire.

BUFFALO CHICKEN
Tater Tot HOTDISH

PREP TIME: 15 MINUTES
COOK TIME: 3–6 HOURS
SERVES 4

If you ever see anything with buffalo sauce in this book or on my blog, know it was made with love for my husband. He literally orders buffalo wings at every place we go out to eat. I usually invent some other way for him to enjoy buffalo chicken so I don't get sick of it. This tater tot hotdish is like a big hug from your loved one on a cold winter day. It is just spicy enough to warm you up without causing you to sweat or your tongue to go numb. Think of a pot-pie filling made of creamy buffalo chicken but with glorious tater tots on top! Eat this with somebody you love who won't judge you for eating half an Instant Pot–ful. Not that that happened or anything . . .

2 tbsp (30 ml) olive oil

1 large boneless, skinless chicken breast, diced

2 tbsp (15 g) Blackening Seasoning Mix (page 168)

1 celery rib, diced

1 carrot, peeled and diced

⅓ cup (50 g) diced red onion

1 cup (240 ml) heavy whipping cream

4 oz (113 g) softened cream cheese, cubed

2 oz (56 g) crumbled blue cheese

½ cup (56 g) shredded mozzarella cheese

½ cup (56 g) shredded sharp cheddar cheese

1½ tbsp (23 ml) buffalo sauce, plus more for serving

1 tbsp (8 g) cornstarch

1 cup (240 ml) whole milk

About 40 frozen tater tots

Fresh chopped cilantro, for garnish

Press "Sauté." Add the olive oil to the Instant Pot along with the chicken and Blackening Seasoning Mix. Mix to combine. Sauté for 5 minutes.

Mix in the celery, carrot and onion. Sauté for 5 more minutes until the onion is translucent.

Mix in the heavy cream and cream cheese. Once the cream cheese melts into the sauce, hit "Cancel."

Stir in the blue cheese, mozzarella, cheddar and buffalo sauce.

Mix the cornstarch with the milk in a separate small bowl. Add the mixture to the Instant Pot and stir to combine. Top the mixture with tater tots.

Secure the lid and leave the steam vent in the open position. Press "Slow Cook," and then use the "−/+" button to adjust the time. Cook for 3 hours on high or 6 hours on low.

Spoon the hotdish out of the Instant Pot into bowls. Top with chopped cilantro and more buffalo sauce.

TEX-MEX CHORIZO *Chilaquiles*

PREP TIME: 10 MINUTES
COOK TIME: 10 MINUTES
OR 3-6 HOURS
SERVES 8

I like to think chilaquiles are the uglier, yet way more fun cousin of nachos. They are a hot mess on the plate but have more to offer than nachos when it comes to flavor. You will love how fun it is to dump a whole bag of tortilla chips into the Instant Pot and call it a meal. You can cook up the saucy mixture ahead of time, keep it on warm and then mix in the chips at the last minute so they don't get too soggy.

1 cup (240 ml) red enchilada sauce

¾ cup (180 ml) BBQ sauce

1 cup (240 ml) low-sodium chicken stock

½ tsp salt

1 canned chipotle pepper, diced

¼ tsp freshly ground black pepper

¼ tsp garlic powder

¼ tsp crushed red pepper flakes

1 lb (450 g) ground pork chorizo

1 cup (150 g) Pinto Bean Tinga (page 141) or Big-Batch Black Beans (page 160)

1 green bell pepper, thinly sliced

1 orange bell pepper, thinly sliced

1 jalapeño, seeded and diced

1 small yellow onion, thinly sliced

13-oz (368-g) bag tortilla chips

¾ cup (85 g) shredded Mexican-blend cheese

¼ cup (30 g) crumbled queso fresco

Fresh chopped cilantro, for garnish

OPTIONAL TOPPINGS
Pico de gallo

Sliced radish

Sliced avocado

Sliced jalapeño

Add the enchilada sauce, BBQ sauce, stock, salt, chipotle pepper, black pepper, garlic powder and crushed red pepper flakes to the Instant Pot. Mix to combine.

Add the chorizo to the pot. Use a wooden spoon to break it apart. Mix in the beans.

Add the bell and jalapeño peppers and onion and mix to combine.

Secure the lid with the steam valve in the sealed position. Press "Pressure Cook" until the light is beneath "High Pressure," and then use the "−/+" button to adjust the time until the display reads 10 minutes.

When the timer is done, quick release the pressure. Remove the lid, and then use the wooden spoon to break up any big pieces of pork.

Add the tortilla chips into the pot, half of the bag at a time, and toss with tongs to evenly coat.

Serve the chilaquiles on a large platter or as individual servings and topped with the shredded Mexican-blend and queso fresco cheeses and cilantro. Pico de gallo, radishes, avocado and more jalapeño are optional toppings.

SLOW COOKER OPTION: Add the chorizo to the pot. Use a wooden spoon to break apart the chorizo. Mix in the beans, peppers and onion until combined. Add the enchilada sauce, BBQ sauce, stock, salt, pepper, garlic powder, chipotle pepper and crushed red pepper to the Instant Pot. Mix to combine. Secure the lid, leaving the steam vent open. Set to "Slow Cook" on high for 3 hours or low for 6 hours. Mix in the chips before serving. Top the chilaquiles accordingly before enjoying.

RED CURRY *Mussels* WITH CHORIZO

PREP TIME: 5 MINUTES
COOK TIME: 3 MINUTES
SERVES 4

This dish was my Father's Day present to my dad. Yep, I gave him one-and-a-half pounds (680 g) of mussels. If that shocks you, you may also be shocked to find out that he ate all of them! Then he soaked up all the sauce with some bread. I hope that speaks volumes to you. These mussels take just ten minutes to make and will have the people you made them for thinking and dreaming about them for WELL over ten minutes.

1 tsp extra-virgin olive oil

½ lb (230 g) ground pork chorizo

1 onion, finely diced

1 jalapeño, seeded and minced

3 cloves garlic, minced

¼ tsp anchovy paste

2 tbsp (28 g) red curry paste

½ cup (120 ml) low-sodium chicken stock

1 tsp salt

¼ tsp freshly ground black pepper

Juice of ½ lime

1½ lbs (680 g) mussels

1 French baguette, sliced, for serving

Press "Sauté" and add the olive oil to the Instant Pot. Wait 1 minute for the oil to heat through. Add the chorizo, onion and jalapeño to the pot. Sauté, stirring and breaking up the chorizo with a wooden spoon, for about 5 minutes.

Add the garlic, anchovy paste and curry paste. Mix to combine. Cook for an additional minute.

Press "Cancel." Add the stock, salt, pepper and lime juice to the pot. Mix to combine, scraping up any bits from the bottom of the pot.

Add in the mussels. Secure the lid with the steam vent closed. Press "Steam." Use the "−/+" button to adjust the time until the display reads 3 minutes.

When the timer is done, quick release the pressure. Remove the lid and discard the mussels that do not open. Transfer the mussels, chorizo and liquid to a large serving bowl.

Serve with some good, crusty bread like a French baguette.

Lil' Quickies: FRENCH ONION CHEESEBURGER SLIDERS

PREP TIME: 12 MINUTES
COOK TIME: 4 HOURS
SERVES 6

Back in the day, I used to be a vegetarian. After a few years of sneaking bites of my boyfriend's (now husband's) cheeseburgers, the lightbulb went off. Cheeseburgers are amazing! I missed them. These are my all-time favorite cheeseburgers. They come together quickly, and the beef crisps up great using the slow-cooking function in the Instant Pot. I know sour cream sounds crazy, but it adds the perfect tang to the burgers that balances out the onion and the cheddar and pickles. I won't fault you if you skip the pickles as long as you don't skip the cheese!

1 lb (450 g) lean ground beef

2 tbsp (5 g) French onion soup seasoning mix

Pinch of salt

Pinch of black pepper

¼ cup (58 g) sour cream

12 brioche slider buns

12 slices cheddar cheese, cut into fourths

12–24 dill pickle slices, optional

Add the beef, French onion seasoning, salt and pepper to the Instant Pot. Use a wooden spoon to break apart the beef the best you can.

Secure the lid and leave the vent open. Set the Instant Pot to "Slow Cook." Press the slow-cook button until it reads "High." Adjust the "–/+" button until the display reads 4 hours.

Once the beef is cooked, remove the lid and break the beef up even further. Mix the sour cream into the beef.

Cut the slider buns in half crosswise. Top the bottom halves with ¼ cup (55 g) scoop of the beef mixture each. Top each scoop of beef with 4 squares of cheddar. Cover with the top halves of the buns and then serve.

This mixture will also hold up well in the refrigerator overnight if you plan on making this ahead of time. Assemble the sliders, cover them with foil and pop them in a 375°F (200°C) oven for 15 minutes or until the cheese melts. Garnish with optional pickles.

MEXICAN COKE & LIME *BBQ Ribs*

PREP TIME: 15 MINUTES, PLUS MARINATING OVERNIGHT
COOK TIME: 12 HOURS OR 30 MINUTES
SERVES 4

My brother is a butcher. When these St. Louis–style ribs were on special, I got many texts from him. He is also the guy who told me to use Mexican Coke because of all the natural sugar. Basically, my brother told me I have to give him all the credit for this recipe. I will, but the cooking method and the dry rub are all me! Slow cooking the ribs makes them super tender and juicy. The steam trivet allows all the fat to drain off and the dry rub to stay crispy on top of the meat. I'd call these ribs the perfect sibling collaboration.

FOR THE MARINADE

12 oz (355 ml) Mexican Coca-Cola

Juice of 1 lime

1 tbsp (8 g) chili powder

1 tsp salt

½ tsp freshly ground black pepper

FOR THE RIBS

1 rack of St. Louis–style spare ribs, cut in half

1 tbsp (8 g) chili powder

1 tsp ground cumin

1 tsp chili-lime seasoning

½ tsp cayenne pepper

½ tsp onion powder

½ tsp garlic powder

½ tsp dried oregano

Zest of 1 lime

1 tsp salt

¼ tsp freshly ground black pepper

¼ cup (60 ml) water

¼ cup (60 ml) apple cider vinegar

Combine the Coca-Cola, lime juice, chili powder, salt and pepper in a 9 × 13-inch (23 × 33-cm) baking pan. Rest the rack of ribs down in the marinade. Cover the ribs with foil and refrigerate overnight.

Remove the ribs from the marinade. Set them off to the side on a baking sheet.

Mix the chili powder, cumin, chili-lime seasoning, cayenne, onion powder, garlic powder, oregano, lime zest, salt and pepper in a small mixing bowl. Sprinkle the seasoning liberally over the top of the ribs. Rub the seasoning into the meat.

Place the steam trivet along with water and the apple cider vinegar into the Instant Pot. Stand the ribs up on the trivet, leaning them against one another.

Secure the lid, leaving the steam vent open. Press "Slow Cook" until the display light is under "Low," and then use the "−/+" button to adjust the time display to read 12 hours. When the timer is done, remove the lid and carefully transfer the ribs to a cutting board. Cut the ribs.

PRESSURE COOKER OPTION: I love slow-cooked ribs, but if you are in a pinch for time, prepare the recipe according to the instructions but cook the ribs at high pressure for 30 minutes. When the timer is done, quick release the steam, remove the lid and then transfer the ribs to a cutting board. Cut the ribs.

CORONA & LIME
Shrimp BOIL

PREP TIME: 15 MINUTES
COOK TIME: 15 MINUTES
SERVES 4

Shrimp is that one member of the seafood family I always forget about. I get cravings for salmon, tilapia and, naturally, fish tacos. But after I make shrimp, I'm like, "Why don't I cook this more often?!?!" It is so easy and cooks up super quick. This shrimp boil highlights everything awesome about shrimp. Using the pressure cooker helps you get all that low and slow-cooked flavor from a traditional shrimp boil in a fraction of the time. Forget the grill, turn on your Instant Pot and invite some friends over. Shrimp's on!

2 ears of corn, shucked and cut into thirds

½ lb (230 g) baby potatoes

½ lb (230 g) baby purple potatoes

1 Vidalia onion, skin removed and quartered

7 oz (202 g) kielbasa, cut into 1-inch (2.5-cm) pieces

½ lemon

½ lime

1 dried bay leaf

1 sprig of fresh thyme

1 tbsp (15 g) salt

1 tsp pepper

¼ tsp cayenne pepper

1 (3-oz [85-g]) bag crab boil seasoning

1 (16-oz [475-ml]) Corona beer

32 oz (950 ml) chicken stock

1½ lbs (680 g) raw deveined pink shrimp

Add the corn, baby potatoes, baby purple potatoes, onion, kielbasa, lemon, lime, bay leaf, thyme, salt, pepper, cayenne and crab boil seasoning bag to the Instant Pot.

Pour the beer and stock over the ingredients. Mix to combine.

Secure the lid and place the vent in the sealed position. Press "Pressure Adjust" to adjust the setting to "high pressure." Use the "−/+" button to change the cook time until the display reads 10 minutes.

When the timer is done, quick release the pressure. Remove the lid. Add the shrimp to the pot. Gently stir and press the shrimp down into the liquid.

Cover with the lid, leaving the vent open. Let the shrimp sit in the hot liquid for 5 minutes, until opaque in color and cooked through.

Remove the shrimp boil contents from the Instant Pot using tongs or a slotted spoon and transfer them to a large serving dish. Discard the bay leaf, thyme stem and seasoning bag before serving.

CLEAN-OUT-THE-FRIDGE *Shakshuka*

When summer rolls around and my dad's garden gets going, I have more produce than I can eat. It is a number one annoyance of mine to have to throw out moldy produce. Once I see that the produce is starting to go, I make a big batch of shakshuka. Normally, shakshuka takes a while to cook because you have to wait for the eggs to slowly, gently poach in the tomato sauce. Not in this case! Spicy tomato sauce with all the vegetables and eggs nestled down inside makes the perfect dinner, lunch or breakfast.

1 zucchini, cut into cubes

1 yellow bell pepper, chopped

1 sweet potato, peeled and cubed

1 onion, diced

3 cloves garlic, minced

1 tsp smoked paprika

1 tsp ground cumin

1 tsp salt

½ tsp freshly ground black pepper

¼ tsp cayenne pepper

Juice of 1 lemon

1 (24-oz [680-g]) can crushed tomatoes

1 cup (240 ml) water

4–6 eggs

½ cup (75 g) crumbled feta

1 tbsp (5 g) fresh chopped parsley

Add the zucchini, bell pepper, sweet potato, onion, garlic, paprika, cumin, salt, pepper, cayenne, lemon juice, tomatoes and water to the Instant Pot. Mix to combine.

Secure the lid with the steam vent closed. Press "Pressure Cook" until the light is underneath "High Pressure." Use the "–/+" button to adjust the time until the display reads 9 minutes.

When the timer is done, quick release the pressure. Remove the lid. Mix the sauce to combine everything. Use a spoon to create a veggie-free area on the surface of the shakshuka, and then crack an egg into that space. Continue until all the eggs have been added to the sauce.

Secure the lid with the steam vent sealed. Press "Pressure Cook" until the light is underneath "High Pressure." Use the "–/+" button to adjust the time until the display reads 1 minute. Once the alert that your Instant Pot is at pressure sounds, press "Cancel," and then quick release the pressure. Remove the lid. The eggs should be cooked through by now.

Top the shakshuka with the feta. Spoon each egg along with some of the sauce and vegetables into a bowl. Top with parsley.

TIP: To make the most of your leftovers, add a Just-Right Jammy Egg (page 159) to any remaining veggies and sauce. Shakshuka round two!

MEYER LEMON POPPY SEED *Chicken* WITH FRESH GREENS

PREP TIME: 10 MINUTES
COOK TIME: 15 MINUTES
SERVES 4

Who says a popular muffin flavor can't translate over to a chicken dish? This is the kind of chicken you want on a salad. This is the kind of salad you make for meal prep to use in other dishes throughout the week. I really love to use chicken cutlets for this—a giant chicken breast would be overkill. This way, all that lemon, poppy seed and sweet-sour flavor is perfectly imparted on the chicken.

¼ cup (60 ml) extra-virgin olive oil

2 tsp (10 ml) plain nonfat Greek yogurt

2 tbsp (30 ml) honey

1 tbsp (15 ml) apple cider vinegar

1 tbsp (15 ml) Meyer lemon juice

½ tsp salt

¼ tsp freshly ground black pepper

¼ tsp ground mustard

½ tsp poppy seeds

4–5 chicken breast cutlets, approximately 1 lb (450 g)

4–5 slices of Meyer lemon

3 cups (90 g) fresh baby spinach or arugula, for serving

To make the sauce, mix the olive oil, yogurt, honey, vinegar, lemon juice, salt, pepper, mustard and poppy seeds together in a small mixing bowl.

Add the chicken cutlets to the Instant Pot. Pour the sauce over the chicken. Cover each chicken cutlet with a slice of Meyer lemon.

Secure the lid, leaving the vent in the closed position. Press "Pressure Cook" until the light is beneath "High Pressure," and then use the "−/+" button to adjust the time display until it reads 15 minutes.

When the timer is done, quick release the pressure. Serve the chicken over a bed of fresh baby spinach or fresh arugula.

Cabbage UN-ROLL UPS

Just like any sane Polish kid, I love a good cabbage roll. Nothing says comfort like a big tray of lovingly and meticulously folded cabbage leaves with beef and rice inside that have been cooked in a beautiful tomato sauce. But, like most people, I DON'T HAVE TIME FOR THAT! I am sure my Polish grandfather is rolling over in his grave after that statement, but for real. I call this a hot mess main dish. It isn't pretty, but it is pure comfort food at its best.

1¼ lbs (563 g) lean ground beef

3 slices of raw bacon, diced

2 tbsp (30 ml) grated onion

½ tsp salt, plus more to taste

¼ tsp freshly ground black pepper, plus more to taste

2 (10.75-oz [305-g]) cans condensed tomato soup

1½ cups (360 ml) low-sodium beef stock

½ head green cabbage, core removed and chopped into 2-inch (5-cm) pieces

½ cup (95 g) jasmine rice

Fresh chopped parsley, for garnish

Press "Sauté" and add the beef, bacon, onion, salt and pepper to the Instant Pot. Use a wooden spoon to break apart the beef. Sauté for 5 minutes.

Press "Cancel" and carefully remove the insert from the Instant Pot using a dish towel or oven mitts. Drain off all the grease in the pot.

Place the insert back into the pot. Mix in the tomato soup, stock and cabbage. Secure the lid, leaving the steam vent open. Press the "Slow Cook" button until the light is beneath "High" and use the "−/+" button to adjust the time to read 3 hours. Or press "Slow Cook" until the display light is beneath "Low" and adjust the time to read 6 hours.

When the cook time display shows there is only 1 hour remaining, remove the lid and mix in the rice. Secure the lid again.

After the hour, remove the lid and taste the mixture. Add more salt and pepper, if needed. Spoon out heaping servings on plates and top with parsley.

PRESSURE COOKER OPTION: Prepare the recipe according to instructions, omitting the rice. After mixing in the cabbage, secure the Instant Pot lid, leaving the steam vent in the closed position. Press "Pressure Cook" and ensure it is set on "High Pressure." Adjust the time to read 20 minutes, and when it's done cooking, quick release the steam. Serve on top of a bed of rice prepared according to package directions.

Lemon-PAPRIKA SMOTHERED PORK CHOPS

PREP TIME: 15 MINUTES
COOK TIME: 45 MINUTES
SERVES 4

One of my mom's famous dishes from our childhood is her pork chops smothered in tomatoes and mushrooms. That big pan of simmering pork chops would cook and cook until the chops fell off the bone. This is my nod to that childhood dish. Or maybe a loooong-distance wave, as I really changed it and made it my own. Using the pressure cooker allows you to get super tender pork chops in half the stovetop time while still extracting all that lemon, smoked paprika and fennel punch of flavor.

3 tbsp (23 g) smoked paprika

½ tsp fennel seed, crushed

½ tsp freshly ground black pepper

1 tsp salt

4¼ lbs (2 kg) boneless pork chops

2 tbsp (30 ml) extra-virgin olive oil

½ lemon

7 oz (202 g) canned fire-roasted diced tomatoes, drained

6 oz (170 g) cremini mushrooms, sliced

⅓ cup (50 g) diced yellow onion

In a small bowl, mix together the paprika, fennel, pepper and salt. Season both sides of each pork chop liberally with the seasoning mixture.

Add the olive oil to the insert in the Instant Pot. Press the "Sauté" button.

Add the pork chops to the Instant Pot, two at a time. Sear on each side for 5 minutes. Transfer the pork chops to a plate.

Hit the "Cancel" button. Add the lemon half, cut side down. Use tongs to grip the lemon. Move the lemon around to deglaze the pot.

Add the tomatoes, mushrooms and onion to the Instant Pot. Nestle the pork chops back into the tomato–mushroom mixture.

Secure the lid and place the steam vent in the sealed position. Press "Pressure Cook." Press "Adjust" to change the pressure to "High Pressure." Hit the "−/+" button until the time display reads 45 minutes.

When the timer is done, natural release pressure for 10 minutes. Quick release any remaining pressure.

Remove the pork chops. Spoon the mushroom–tomato mixture over the pork chops.

GREEK HERB & FETA *Clams*

PREP TIME: 5 MINUTES
COOK TIME: 3 MINUTES
SERVES 4

Perfectly tender clams in a white wine and lemon-butter sauce has date night written all over it. Lucky for you, the trip to the store for these ingredients takes longer than steaming up these clams. I live for meals that make it look like I worked way harder than I did. I know you will too after the first time you make these clams.

⅓ cup (80 ml) dry white wine

1 lemon, halved

Pinch of salt

2 tbsp (30 g) unsalted butter

1 clove garlic, grated

2 tsp (6 g) capers

1½–2 lbs (680–907 g) little neck clams (about 20)

1 tsp fresh chopped oregano

1 tsp fresh chopped Italian flat-leaf parsley

½ tsp fresh chopped basil

½ tsp fresh chopped dill

Freshly ground black pepper

¼ cup (38 g) feta crumbles

Noodles, rice or bread, for serving

Add the wine, lemon halves, salt, butter, garlic, capers and clams to the Instant Pot.

Secure the lid, with the steam valve sealed. Press "Steam," and then use the "−/+" button to adjust the time until the display reads 3 minutes.

When the timer is up, quick release the pressure. Remove the lid.

Add the oregano, parsley, basil and dill, and then squeeze out the remaining juice from the lemon halves using tongs.

Transfer the clams and all the cooking liquid to a large serving bowl. Discard any clams that do not open. Top with the pepper and the crumbled feta and and serve with noodles, rice or a good loaf of bread.

Korean BBQ BEEF LETTUCE WRAPS

When I was testing this recipe for the book, I allowed Mike only one bite. I had to ensure the carnivore in the family liked the beef. Then I hid the rest in the back of the fridge. I ate these for three days straight. I was able to eat them in front of Mike because they were wrapped up in his archnemesis, lettuce.

1¼ lbs (563 g) lean ground beef

¼ cup (55 g) light brown sugar, lightly packed

1 tbsp (15 ml) rice wine or apple cider vinegar

1 tsp chili paste

1 tsp sesame oil

½ cup (120 ml) low-sodium soy sauce

½ tsp salt

½ tsp freshly ground black pepper

4 cloves garlic, grated

½ tsp freshly grated ginger

8–12 butter lettuce leaves

4 green onions, thinly sliced, for garnish

½ cup (65 g) carrot matchsticks, for garnish

Sesame seeds, for garnish

Press "Sauté" and add the beef to the Instant Pot. Cook for about 5 minutes, breaking up the beef with a wooden spoon. After 5 minutes, press "Cancel." Carefully remove the insert using a kitchen towel or oven mitts and drain off the excess grease.

Mix in the brown sugar, rice wine, chili paste, sesame oil, soy sauce, salt, pepper, garlic and ginger.

Secure the lid with the vent sealed. Press "Pressure Cook" until the Instant Pot is set to "High Pressure." Use the "–/+" button to adjust the time until the display reads 10 minutes. When the timer is done, quick release the pressure. Remove the lid and mix the beef.

Arrange the lettuce leaves on a plate and top them with a few spoonfuls of the beef mixture. Top with the green onions, carrot and sesame seeds.

EVERYTHING BAGEL, CREAM CHEESE, SAUSAGE & EGG *Casserole*

PREP TIME: 7 MINUTES,
PLUS SOAKING OVERNIGHT
COOK TIME: 20 MINUTES
SERVES 4

Ever since Trader Joe's came out with its everything seasoning blend, I've been finding ways to incorporate a sprinkle of it on everything. It is seriously every flavor you would ever want on anything. EVER! Especially this casserole. The bagels soak up the egg, cream cheese and milk mixture overnight, and when you steam them up in the Instant Pot, the bagels get all puffed up and turn into a super creamy, savory bread pudding. You are going to love this close runner-up to my favorite recipe in the book.

7 large eggs

½ cup (120 ml) whole milk

½ tsp salt

¼ tsp freshly ground black pepper

¼ cup (31 g) freshly shredded white cheddar

Butter, for greasing the dish

2 everything bagels, cut into 1-inch (2.5-cm) pieces

½ cup (75 g) cooked sausage crumbles

2 oz (57 g) cream cheese

½ tsp everything bagel seasoning blend

1 cup (240 ml) water

1 green onion, chopped, for garnish

Whisk together the eggs, milk, salt, pepper and cheddar in a medium mixing bowl.

Grease a 20-ounce (567-g), 7-inch (18-cm) circular baking dish with the butter. Add the cut bagels and sausage to the prepared dish. Pour the egg mixture over the bagels. Cover with little pinches of cream cheese and the everything bagel seasoning. Cover the dish with plastic wrap and place in the fridge overnight.

Place the water along with the steam trivet into the Instant Pot. Place the baking dish on the trivet.

Secure the lid and close the steam vent. Press "Pressure Cook" until the display light is underneath "High Pressure." Use the "−/+" button to change the time until the display reads 20 minutes.

When the timer is done, quick release the steam. Carefully remove the baking dish. Garnish with the green onion.

Pineapple BUFFALO CHICKEN WINGS

PREP TIME: 15 MINUTES
COOK TIME: 5 MINUTES
SERVES 4-6

I am the person in your life who loves finding ways to add pineapple to everything. You know, the person who will say, "I love pineapple on pizza!" Well, that's me! Yay! My husband was thrilled to learn that I had added lovely tart pineapple to his beloved chicken wings. I told him only after he ate a whole dozen so he couldn't protest. Wings get super tender rather quickly in the Instant Pot. I like to broil them for a minute or two to crisp them up right before I serve them. People will think you put way more time and effort into this recipe than you actually did. What they don't know won't hurt them.

2 lbs (907 g) chicken wings, drumettes and wingettes only

1 tsp cornstarch

1 tsp Blackening Seasoning Mix (page 168)

½ cup (120 ml) water

½ cup (120 ml) buffalo sauce

1 tsp honey

¼ cup (50 g) canned crushed pineapple

½ tsp salt

¼ tsp freshly ground black pepper

Toss the chicken wings, cornstarch and Blackening Seasoning Mix together in a medium mixing bowl using tongs.

Add the water plus the steam trivet to the Instant Pot.

Layer the chicken wings on top of the steam trivet. Secure the lid, placing the steam vent in the closed position. Press "Pressure Cook" until the display light is beneath "High Pressure." Use the "−/+" button to adjust the time until the display reads 5 minutes.

While the wings cook, add the buffalo sauce, honey, pineapple, salt and pepper to a food processor. Puree until smooth.

Allow the Instant Pot's pressure to release naturally for 5 minutes, and then quick release the remaining steam.

Remove the chicken wings from the Instant Pot and transfer them to a baking sheet lined with foil or parchment paper.

Set the broiler to high. Baste each wing with a healthy amount of the prepared sauce.

Broil the wings until crisp and golden, about 3 to 4 minutes.

TIP: To save time when you get home, ask your butcher to break down the store's prepackaged chicken wings into the drumette, wingette and wing tip if they aren't already separated. Freeze the wing tips to make stock later.

Turkey EGG ROLL, MEATBALLS

PREP TIME: 10 MINUTES
COOK TIME: 6–12 HOURS
SERVES 4–6

Growing up, we ate a lot of Chinese food. There was nothing better than diving into all the little boxes and ripping your specific order out of your siblings' hands. Or is that just me? I always wondered why some places gave you only two egg rolls in each order; in our family, we would have to order two for each person! I devised this recipe to re-create the egg roll flavors at home with enough for everybody. Juicy turkey with cabbage, carrots, garlic, ginger and a kick of red pepper really evoke that egg roll filling even without the deep frying and wonton.

FOR THE SAUCE

¼ cup (60 ml) vegetable stock

2 tsp (5 g) cornstarch

⅓ cup (80 ml) low-sodium soy sauce

Juice of 1 orange

1 tsp Worcestershire sauce

1 tsp sriracha sauce

¼ cup (60 ml) honey

1 tsp sesame oil

1 tsp minced garlic

1 green onion, chopped

¼ tsp freshly ground black pepper

FOR THE MEATBALLS

6 oz (170 g) coleslaw blend of carrots, cabbage and red cabbage (about 2 cups)

1 lb (450 g) 93% lean ground turkey

1 egg white

½ tsp salt

¼ tsp freshly ground black pepper

1 tsp minced garlic

½ tsp grated ginger

Pinch of crushed red pepper flakes

GARNISH

Sesame seeds

Chopped green onion

Fried wonton strips

Combine the stock and cornstarch in a measuring cup. Mix until the cornstarch has fully dissolved.

Add the cornstarch slurry along with the soy sauce, orange juice, Worcestershire, sriracha, honey, sesame oil, garlic, green onion and pepper to the bowl of a slow cooker. Whisk well to combine.

Add the coleslaw blend to a food processor. Pulse 3 to 4 times until the blend is finely chopped. Transfer the coleslaw blend to a medium mixing bowl. Add the ground turkey, egg white, salt, pepper, garlic, ginger and red pepper flakes. Mix to combine.

Form the meat mixture into balls about ¼ cup (55 g) in size, 16 to 20 total. Transfer the formed meatballs to the Instant Pot.

Place the lid on the Instant Pot. Set the slow-cooker function to high for 6 hours or low for 12. About halfway through, or at least once during the cooking process, open the lid and give the meatballs a stir.

Once the meatballs are completely cooked through, remove them using tongs and transfer each meatball to a large serving dish or bowl.

Place a fine-mesh strainer over the serving bowl containing the meatballs. Whisk the sauce in the pot a few times to loosen any browned bits. Using oven mitts, lift the insert out of the unit and dump the sauce through the strainer.

Serve the meatballs on their own, in a mini sub sandwich or with brown rice. Garnish them with a little extra sauce, sesame seeds, green onion and fried wonton strips.

TIP: This recipe can double as an appetizer in a pinch. Strain the sauce, then transfer everything back to the Instant Pot. Keep it on warm and serve the meatballs with toothpicks and garnishes.

BLACKENED WHOLE FAUX-STED *Chicken*

PREP TIME: 10 MINUTES,
PLUS REFRIGERATING OVERNIGHT
COOK TIME: 35 MINUTES
SERVES 4

My pug, Weezer, is my number one fan—mainly because I feed him. He will literally sit next to the warm oven all day long and wait for a roasted chicken to finish in hopes of a few scraps being tossed his way. A few great things about making a roasted or faux-sted chicken in the Instant Pot: It's quick, slightly spicy, fall-off-the-bone tender and doesn't heat up your entire house. By the time the beeps from the Instant Pot sound and Weezer realizes what that means, I put the chicken into its serving dish and out of his sight. But I'm a sucker, so I still save a few bites for him.

1 (3- to 4-lb [1.3- to 1.8-kg]) whole chicken, innards removed

1 tbsp (15 g) unsalted butter

2 tbsp (30 ml) extra-virgin olive oil, divided

3 tbsp (23 g) Blackening Seasoning Mix (page 168)

½ lemon

Small handful of fresh parsley

½ cup (120 ml) water

Remove the chicken from its packaging. Pat it dry using paper towels. Set the chicken on a baking sheet topped with a wire rack. Put the chicken in the fridge overnight to dry out.

Rub the chicken all over with the butter and 1 tablespoon (15 ml) of olive oil. Loosen the skin over the breasts and rub some olive oil and butter under there too. Season the chicken liberally with the Blackening Seasoning Mix. Place the lemon half and parsley inside the chicken cavity.

Set the Instant Pot to "Sauté." Add the other tablespoon (15 ml) of olive oil to the Instant Pot. Add the whole chicken, breast side down. Sear the chicken for 7 minutes.

After 7 minutes, hit "Cancel," remove the chicken and transfer it to a plate. Add the water to the pot along with the steam rack.

Truss the legs together with kitchen twine. Add the chicken back into the Instant Pot by placing it on the steamer rack. Press the "Pressure Cook" button. Adjust to "High Pressure." Press the "−/+" button until the display screen reads 35 minutes.

When the timer is done, quick release the pressure. Carefully remove the steamer rack with the chicken still on it. Let the chicken cool for 5 minutes before cutting and serving.

MY REUBEN *Semi-Sliders*

PREP TIME: 15 MINUTES
COOK TIME: 12 HOURS
SERVES 4–6

Remember looking at foods your parents ate while you were still a kid and thinking "huh"? This recipe was that for me. I just never really knew what it was. Pinkish meat, but is it beef? It took me years to finally try a Reuben. What was I waiting for? Slow-cooked corned beef with a little Thousand Island crust on the edges is piled high with sauerkraut and melty Swiss cheese. Now that I actually know what is inside this sandwich, I want it all the time. Each bite basically says, "Congrats! You're an adult!"

2½ lbs (1.2 kg) corned beef brisket, plus seasoning packet

¼ cup (60 ml) Thousand Island dressing, plus more for serving

Pinch of salt

¼ tsp black pepper

10–12 slices Jewish rye mini-loaf

10–12 slices Swiss cheese

2 cups (284 g) sauerkraut

Remove the corned beef from its packaging. Drain all the liquid and pat the beef dry.

Place the corned beef into the Instant Pot. Coat the top of the corned beef with the ¼ cup (60 ml) Thousand Island dressing and the salt, pepper and seasoning packet.

Secure the lid, leave the vent open and press the "Slow Cook" button until the display light is beneath "Low." Use the "–/+" button to adjust the time until the display reads 12 hours.

Once the meat is fully cooked, add the bread slices to a large baking sheet. Place under the broiler in the oven to toast the bread for 2 to 3 minutes.

Flip the bread and add the Swiss cheese to half of the bread slices, folding to fit the slices. Toast under the broiler for 2 more minutes.

Carefully remove the beef from the Instant Pot and transfer it to a plate. Trim off any fat. Shred the beef and add about 5 ounces (142 g) of beef to each slice of bread without cheese. Top with the sauerkraut and more Thousand Island dressing, and then top with a bread slice with melted cheese. Cut the sliders in half.

Chicago POLISH SAUSAGES

PREP TIME: 4 MINUTES
COOK TIME: 3-8 HOURS
SERVES 3-6

Having your first Chicago-style hot dog is a rite of passage here in Illinois. Once I had that crazy topping combination of mustard, tomatoes, pickles, neon green relish, diced onion, sport peppers and celery salt all on a poppy-seed bun, I could not ever go back. I wanted to do a slow-cooked Polish sausage nod to the Chicago dog. These guys are cooked in beer and topped with another local favorite: giardiniera. They're always and only ever topped with yellow mustard and never ketchup. But if you wanna throw a little ketchup on top, no judgment.

1 yellow onion, thinly sliced

6 oz (180 ml) light-colored beer or ale

6 Polish sausages (about 16 oz [450 g])

6 poppy-seed buns

1 cup (150 g) hot giardiniera, drained

Yellow mustard

Add the onion, beer and sausages to the Instant Pot. Secure the lid and leave the vent open.

Press the "Slow Cook" button until the display light is under "Low." Hit the "–/+" button until the time display reads 8 hours.

When the time is up, place the cooked sausages onto the poppy-seed buns. Top each with some of the beer-caramelized onions from the Instant Pot along with the giardiniera and a squirt of yellow mustard.

TIP: Polish sausages can also be cooked on "High" for 3 hours.

Feisty SLOPPY JOEYS

Truth be told, we were never a sloppy joe kind of family while growing up. However, as an adult, I have made them on multiple occasions for Mike and myself. And I looove them! My version is spicy with hot giardiniera, ground beef and Italian sausage. I like to think my recipe is modeled after Joey from _Friends_. It is a little bit spicy and messy, very easy but irresistible. My kids don't eat it, but I don't mind. More for Mike and me!

1 lb (450 g) lean ground beef

1 lb (450 g) mild ground Italian sausage

½ green bell pepper, diced

½ yellow onion, diced

1 tsp salt, plus more to taste

½ tsp freshly ground black pepper, plus more to taste

½ tsp minced garlic

½ tsp dried oregano

¾ cup (110 g) chopped hot (or mild) giardiniera

2 cups (475 ml) Tomato-Garlic Sauce (page 167)

6 oz (180 ml) tomato paste

8 whole-wheat hamburger buns, sliced and toasted

8 slices of mozzarella cheese

Add the beef, Italian sausage, bell pepper, onion, salt, pepper, garlic, oregano, giardiniera and Tomato-Garlic Sauce to the Instant Pot. Mix to combine evenly.

Secure the lid with the vent in the sealed position. Press "Pressure Cook" until the light is beneath "High Pressure." Use the "−/+" button to adjust the time until the display reads 20 minutes.

When the timer is done, quick release the pressure. Remove the lid and mix in the tomato paste. Add more salt and pepper to taste.

Place about a ¾ cup (165 g) scoop of meat on each bottom bun half. Top with a slice of cheese and the top bun half. Allow the cheese to slightly melt before serving.

SLOW COOKER OPTION: Add the beef, Italian sausage, bell pepper, onion, salt, pepper, garlic, oregano, giardiniera, Tomato-Garlic Sauce and tomato paste to the Instant Pot. Mix to combine evenly. Secure the lid with the steam vent open. Press "Slow Cook" and ensure the light beneath "High" is on. Adjust the time display to read 3 hours.

SPED-UP CLASSIC CHIPOTLE
Carnitas Tacos

PREP TIME: 15 MINUTES
COOK TIME: 1 HOUR 20 MINUTES
SERVES 4–6

I love slow-cooker carnitas. That in fact is the only way I ever cook them. Low and slow. That fat cooks off and bathes the rest of the pork shoulder in juices until the pork crisps up. I never believed the Instant Pot pressure-cooking setting could get those exact results—that is, until I started making this recipe. I will never go back, mainly out of laziness and a lack of time. If it works, why mess with it, right?

4 lbs (1.8 kg) bone-in pork shoulder, cut into 3 pieces

1 tbsp (15 g) salt

1 tsp freshly ground black pepper

2 tsp (8 g) ground cumin

3 cloves garlic, smashed and cut in half

2 tbsp (30 ml) olive oil

Juice of 1 orange

1 yellow onion, thinly sliced

1 jalapeño, sliced

1–2 tbsp (10–20 g) chipotle-adobo puree

1 bay leaf

8–12 tortillas, corn or flour

Season each side of the pork shoulder pieces liberally with salt, pepper and cumin. Use a sharp knife to make two 1-inch (2.5-cm) slits down into each piece of pork. Nestle half of a garlic clove halfway down into each slit.

On the Instant Pot, press "Sauté." Add the olive oil and swirl the pot around to evenly coat the bottom. Add the three pieces of pork. Sear on each side for about 10 minutes total.

Hit "Cancel." Remove the meat and transfer it to a plate. Add the orange juice to the pot and scrape off any bits of pork stuck to the bottom.

Add the onion, jalapeño and pork pieces back to the pot. Use a spoon to spread the chipotle-adobo puree over the top of each piece of pork.

Add the bay leaf to the pot. Secure the lid and close the steam vent. Press "Pressure Cook" until the light is underneath "High Pressure." Use the "–/+" button to change the time display to read 1 hour and 20 minutes.

When the timer is done, allow the pressure to natural release for 10 minutes. Quick release the remaining pressure.

Remove the lid. Remove the fat from the pork along with the bone and the bay leaf. Use two forks to shred the pork in the pot. Add about 4 to 5 ounces (113 to 142 g) of pork to each tortilla and top with whatever you desire!

RANCH-SEASONED *Steaks* & POTATOES

PREP TIME: 7 MINUTES
COOK TIME: 7 MINUTES
SERVES 4

Yes! Steak and potatoes in one pot. You read that right. I had Mike make this recipe for me when I was working on the book. It was basically my way of showing him that it is so easy to make a fancy date-night meal in much less than 30 minutes. Hint, hint. Sear the steaks and then let them rest while you cook the potatoes in the beef juices. It doesn't get any better. And if he can do it, so can you!

4½ lbs (2 kg) filet mignon steaks, at room temperature

3 tbsp (23 g) ranch dressing seasoning mix

Salt, to taste

Black pepper, to taste

2 tbsp (30 g) unsalted butter

1 clove garlic, minced

¼ cup (60 ml) dry white wine or beef stock

¾ lb (340 g) baby potatoes, cut in half

8 oz (230 g) frozen broccoli florets, optional

Chopped fresh chives, for garnish

Pat each steak dry with paper towels. Season each side liberally with the ranch seasoning, salt and pepper.

Set the Instant Pot to "Sauté." Once the display reads "Hot," add the seasoned steaks. Sear for 4 minutes. Add the butter and garlic to the Instant Pot. Flip and sear the steaks for an additional 4 minutes for medium steaks. If you like a more well-done steak, sear for 6 to 7 minutes on each side. For a rarer steak, sear for 2 to 3 minutes on the second side.

Spoon the melted garlic butter all over the steaks as the second sides sear.

Remove the steaks, set them on a plate, tent them with foil and let them rest while you cook the potatoes.

Deglaze the pot with the wine or stock. Add the potatoes and broccoli, if using, and mix to scrape up all the burnt bits from the bottom of the pan. Turn off the sauté function.

Secure the lid. Close the steam valve. Press "Pressure Cook." Adjust the pressure level to "High Pressure." Press the "−/+" button until the display reads 7 minutes. Once the timer is done, quick release the steam. Plate the steaks along with the potatoes. Top everything with fresh chopped chives.

TIP: Toss in some frozen or fresh broccoli with the potatoes for a little bit of extra veggies. They really soak up all the delicious cooking liquid.

BOURBON POT ROAST *Nachos*

PREP TIME: 15 MINUTES
COOK TIME: 1 HOUR
SERVES 4-6

When I am jonesing for a nacho fix, I love to pressure cook this bourbon pot roast until it is so tender it's falling apart. It is spicy, sweet and juicy, which makes it perfect for loading a tortilla chip.

FOR THE POT ROAST
2½ lb (1.2 kg) chuck-eye beef roast

1 tbsp (15 g) salt

1 tsp freshly ground black pepper

1 tsp onion powder

1 tbsp (15 ml) olive oil

FOR THE BOURBON GLAZE
¼ cup (60 ml) red wine

⅓ cup (80 ml) bourbon

2 tbsp (30 g) ketchup

¼ tsp thyme

1 tsp salt

½ tsp freshly ground black pepper

1 tbsp (15 ml) maple syrup

1 tbsp (15 ml) Worcestershire sauce

½ tsp grated horseradish

2 cloves garlic, grated

FOR THE NACHOS
8 oz (230 g) tortilla chips

¾ cup (110 g) Big-Batch Black Beans (page 160)

2 cups (450 g) shredded bourbon pot roast meat

1½ cups (170 g) shredded sharp cheddar cheese

½ cup (56 g) shredded mozzarella cheese

1 jalapeño, sliced

2 green onions, chopped

½ cup (90 g) diced tomatoes

Chopped fresh cilantro, for garnish

Use paper towels to blot the roast dry. Season all sides of the roast with salt, pepper and onion powder.

Whisk together the red wine, bourbon, ketchup, thyme, salt, pepper, maple syrup, Worcestershire, horseradish and garlic in a small mixing bowl.

Add the olive oil to the Instant Pot. Press "Sauté," and then add the seasoned beef to the Instant Pot.

Sear on all sides for about 10 minutes total. Remove the beef and transfer it to a plate off to the side.

Press "Cancel," and then deglaze the Instant Pot with half of the bourbon glaze. Use a wooden spoon to scrape all the charred beef bits off the bottom of the pot.

Place the roast back into the pot. Pour the remaining glaze over the beef. Secure the lid, placing the steam vent in the closed position. Press "Pressure Cook" until the light is beneath "High Pressure." Use the "−/+" button to set the time display to 60 minutes.

Once the timer is done, quick release the pressure. Remove the lid. Use two forks to shred the beef and mix it with the sauce.

Arrange the tortilla chips on a baking sheet. Top with the beans and three-quarters of the beef. Cover with the cheddar, mozzarella and remaining beef. Place under a high broiler in the oven for 5 minutes.

Remove the nachos when the cheese is melted. Top with the jalapeño, green onions, tomatoes and cilantro.

COMFORTING CARBS

From the recipes listed in the table of contents, you have probably identified some of my favorite foods. You can see I totally favor Mexican cuisine—taco night is clearly not optional in our house. The other night that makes a regular occurrence is pasta night, or noodle night.

Noodles are always comforting to me, which is why I generally make noodle night a Monday. It is a good way to ease into the week ahead. You also generally have few naysayers with a giant bowl of pasta on the table. Even my picky toddler loves noodles.

Noodles are super versatile too! They can be fancy and a showstopper, such as the Red Wine Short Rib Ziti (page 67) and the Chili, Lobster & Vodka Linguine (page 64). They can be a meal of pure comfort pulled from your childhood, like the Turkey Burger Helper with Peas (page 88). Noodles can also be a great vehicle for all the crazy-good flavor combo ideas that live in my head, which is what happened with the Green Chili Macaroni & Pimento Cheese (page 72).

In this section you will find a wide range of the easiest, quickest and most flavorful one-pot noodle dishes you will ever need! They'll make the days of waiting for water to boil a distant memory!

CHILI, LOBSTER & VODKA *Linguine*

PREP TIME: 10 MINUTES
COOK TIME: 8 MINUTES
SERVES 4

Lobster is usually reserved for special occasions in my book. It can be daunting to prepare a surf-and-turf meal for that special person or people. This is the dish to make the next time a situation like that arises. Toss it all in the Instant Pot and end up with the most buttery noodles and perfectly steamed lobster tails. Instant love and appreciation for the Instant Pot.

1 large tomato, diced

1 lb (450 g) linguine, cracked in half

1 tsp salt, plus more to taste

¼ tsp freshly ground black pepper, plus more to taste

2 tsp (10 ml) chili sauce

¼ cup (60 ml) vodka

⅓ cup (80 ml) lemon juice

2¾ cups (655 ml) water

4 lobster tails, cut in half lengthwise using kitchen shears

2 tbsp (30 g) unsalted butter

1 tsp fresh chopped parsley, for garnish

1 tsp fresh chopped basil, for garnish

Add the diced tomato, linguine, salt, pepper, chili sauce, vodka, lemon juice and water to the Instant Pot. Mix and toss with tongs to distribute the ingredients. Top with the lobster tails.

Secure the lid, leaving the vent in the closed position. Press "Pressure Cook," making sure the light is beneath "High Pressure." Use the "−/+" button to adjust the time until the display reads 8 minutes.

Once the noodles are cooked, quick release the steam. Remove the lid and use tongs to transfer the lobster tails to a plate.

Toss the linguine with the butter, parsley and basil. Add more salt and pepper to taste. Remove the insert from the Instant Pot so the noodles have a chance to start cooling down and do not continue to cook from the residual heat in the Instant Pot.

Pull the lobster meat out of the tails, roughly chop it and then return it to the noodles. Toss to combine.

TIP: The lobster tails can be served in their shells for a fancier presentation.

RED WINE
Short Rib ZITI

PREP TIME: 10 MINUTES
COOK TIME: 55 MINUTES
SERVES 4-6

Any time a holiday, birthday or special occasion rolls around and I am in charge of cooking, I always go to short ribs cooked in red wine. I normally wake up really early, sear the short ribs and get the whole dish in the oven for a good eight to ten hours. Short ribs are always a showstopper if you have the time to wait for them to cook until they fall apart. I found a way to get that same slow-roasted, fall-off-the-bone quality in a fraction of the time. It is up to you whether you want to tell everybody how you made this dish.

1 tsp extra-virgin olive oil

2 lbs (907 g) bone-in beef short ribs (about 4 ribs)

1 tbsp (15 g) salt, plus more for seasoning

½ tsp freshly ground black pepper, plus more for seasoning

1 onion, finely diced

1 celery stalk, diced

1 carrot, grated

3 cloves garlic, minced

1½ cups (360 ml) dry red wine

3 oz (85 g) tomato paste

1 (28-oz [794-g]) can crushed tomatoes

28 oz (825 ml) water

1 tsp dried basil

1 tsp dried oregano

Pinch of crushed red pepper flakes

10 oz (283 g) dry ziti

Grated Parmesan cheese, for topping

Add the olive oil to the Instant Pot. Press "Sauté" and wait about 2 to 3 minutes for the Instant Pot to get hot.

Season the short ribs with a little salt and pepper. Add them to the pot and sear on both sides for a total of 6 minutes. Press "Cancel" and remove the short ribs from the pot. Drain off half of the rendered fat.

Add the onion, celery, carrot and garlic to the pot. Stir and scrape off any burnt bits from the bottom of the pot.

Add the wine. Continue scraping the bottom of the pot. Mix in the tomato paste.

Once the tomato paste has been fully incorporated into the wine, add the can of crushed tomatoes. Pour the water right into the empty tomato can, and then add that to the pot as well.

Mix in the salt, pepper, basil, oregano and red pepper flakes. Add the short ribs back to the Instant Pot.

Secure the lid and seal the steam vent. Press "Meat/Stew." Use the "−/+" button to adjust the time until the display reads 55 minutes.

Once the short ribs are cooked, quick release the pressure. Remove the lid and carefully transfer the short ribs to a plate. Discard the bones and use two forks to shred the beef.

Add the ziti to the pot, stirring to combine. Press "Sauté" until the display light is under "Less." Let the ziti cook for 10 to 12 minutes until tender.

Add the short ribs back to the pot. Stir to combine. Press "Cancel."

Serve topped with the grated Parmesan.

Lemon CACIO E PEPE

PREP TIME: 5 MINUTES
COOK TIME: 6 MINUTES
SERVES 4

The great thing about written recipes is that you do not get to hear my sad attempts at proper food pronunciations. It is probably for the best—fewer people to offend. As for you guys, sorry. You're on your own. I'll give you a tip though: Just call this Parmesan-lemon-pepper pasta, and people will know what you're talking about.

Regardless of pronunciation, adding the lemon component to this simple dish is a little tweak that brings big flavor. Cooking this dish in the Instant Pot allows all that flavor to be sucked into the noodles.

1 lb (450 g) dry spaghetti

½ tsp salt

2½ cups (600 ml) water

1 tbsp (15 ml) olive oil

½ cup (120 ml) lemon juice

1 cup (8-oz [224-g]) freshly grated Parmesan cheese, plus more for topping

Zest of 1 lemon

1 tsp freshly ground black pepper, plus more for topping

Crack the spaghetti noodles in half so they will easily fit in the Instant Pot. Add the noodles along with the salt, water and olive oil to the pot. Give the noodles a good mix; this will help prevent the noodles from sticking together later.

Secure the lid and close the pressure valve. Set the Instant Pot to manual high pressure for 6 minutes.

Once the noodles are cooked, quick release the steam and turn the Instant Pot off. Remove the lid and give the noodles a stir and toss using tongs.

Add the lemon juice, Parmesan, lemon zest and black pepper. Toss to evenly coat.

Transfer the noodles to plates. Top with a little more Parmesan and black pepper. Serve right away.

TIP: To reheat leftovers, add a tablespoon (15 ml) of water to the noodles and microwave for 1 to 2 minutes until hot.

BALSAMIC BURST TOMATO & BASIL *Bucatini*

PREP TIME: 5 MINUTES
COOK TIME: 9 MINUTES
SERVES 4–6

Based on the ingredient list, there isn't much to this dish. Yet if you ask me, this is what I would want for dinner every day. Sometimes, all you need to make a winning dish is some fresh tomatoes, good noodles and a multi-cooker to bring it all together and infuse those noodles with all that tomato and vinegar flavor.

2½ cups (600 ml) water

½ tsp salt, plus more to taste

1 tbsp (15 ml) balsamic vinegar

1 tsp olive oil

¼ tsp freshly ground black pepper, plus more to taste

16 oz (450 g) dry bucatini pasta noodles, cracked in half

24 oz (680 g) cherry or grape tomatoes

Fresh basil, chopped, for serving

Grated Parmesan cheese, for topping

Add the water, salt, vinegar, olive oil, pepper and noodles to the Instant Pot. Mix with tongs to combine. Top the noodles with the tomatoes.

Secure the Instant Pot lid with the vent in the sealed position. Press "Pressure Cook" until the light is beneath "High Pressure." Use the "–/+" button to adjust the time until the display reads 9 minutes.

When the noodles are cooked, quick release the pressure, remove the lid and toss the noodles with tongs. Use the tongs to gently burst any tomato that has not burst on its own yet.

Add more salt and pepper to taste.

Serve the noodles with fresh chopped basil and grated Parmesan on top.

GREEN CHILI *Macaroni* & PIMENTO CHEESE

PREP TIME: 10 MINUTES
COOK TIME: 5 MINUTES
SERVES 4–6

Throughout the creation of this book, this recipe has been my favorite. Hands down. There's something about the pimento cheese that is just meant to be sauce for mac and cheese. Pimento cheese is a mixture of mayo, cheddar cheese, pimentos and Worcestershire sauce. It is normally served on crackers as a dip in the South. I am pretty sure my Southern friends with Southern mamas would be proud of this dish because it sets pimento cheese on a pedestal and makes one heck of a creamy mac and cheese in fifteen minutes.

FOR THE PIMENTO CHEESE

8 oz (230 g) sharp cheddar cheese, finely grated

½ cup (110 g) mayonnaise

¼ tsp Worcestershire sauce

1 (4-oz [113-g]) jar pimento peppers, drained and finely chopped

FOR THE MAC AND CHEESE

16 oz (450 g) dry macaroni noodles

2 cups (475 ml) low-sodium chicken stock

1¾ cups (420 ml) water

¼ tsp freshly ground black pepper, plus more to taste

¼ tsp ground cumin

¼ tsp smoked paprika

¼ tsp garlic powder

¼ tsp ground mustard

½ tsp salt, plus more to taste

1 (4-oz [113-g]) can diced mild green chilies

1 cup (113 g) shredded mozzarella

1 jalapeño, seeded and diced, divided

To prepare the pimento cheese, mix the cheddar, mayonnaise, Worcestershire and pimentos together in a small bowl. Cover with plastic wrap and place in the refrigerator until the noodles are cooked.

Mix together the dry noodles, stock, water, pepper, cumin, paprika, garlic powder, mustard, salt and green chilies in the Instant Pot.

Secure the lid and set the vent to the sealed position. Press "Pressure Cook." Adjust the pressure to "High Pressure." Press the "–/+" button until the time display reads 5 minutes.

Once the timer sounds, quick release the pressure. Remove the pimento cheese from the fridge and mix it into the noodles along with the mozzarella and half of the diced jalapeño.

Season with more salt and pepper to taste. Garnish with the remaining diced jalapeño.

NOTE: The sauce will thicken up as the macaroni cools.

CITRUS-HERB *Cod* WITH VEGGIE NOODLES

PREP TIME: 10 MINUTES
COOK TIME: 9 MINUTES
SERVES 4

I know, I know: These aren't really noodles. But sometimes you need to trick your mind and body by subbing in some good vegetables instead of carbs every now and then. Throw some good olive oil and a ton of herbs plus citrus on anything, and I will devour it. This healthy and delicious meal is all steamed in one little convenient pouch. Use a fork to squeeze out all that citrus, and break apart the fish so you can have a bite with each "noodle." Bring on that second glass of wine!

1 medium zucchini, spiralized

1 small sweet potato, spiralized

2-lb (907-g) cod fillet, cut into 4 portions

4 tsp (20 ml) basil-infused olive oil, divided (extra-virgin works too)

½ tsp salt

1 tsp smoked paprika

½ tsp lemon pepper

1 tsp fresh chopped dill

1 tsp fresh chopped oregano

4 orange slices

2 grapefruit slices, cut in half

4 lemon slices

4 lime slices

4 fresh thyme sprigs

1 cup (240 ml) water

Prepare four 12 × 12-inch (30 × 30-cm) square pieces of parchment paper.

Divide the zucchini noodles and the sweet potato noodles equally between the four pieces of parchment.

Top the noodles with the pieces of cod. Drizzle each piece of fish with a teaspoon of olive oil. Season each piece of fish with equal amounts of the salt, paprika and lemon pepper. Sprinkle the dill and oregano over each piece of fish as well.

Top each piece of fish with a slice of orange, grapefruit, lemon and lime. Tuck a thyme sprig in between the slices of fruit.

Fold in one edge of paper toward the center, and then do the same with the opposite side. Take the two remaining edges and bring them into the center. Fold those two pieces down toward the fish, forming a little pouch. Continue until all the pouches have been made.

Add the water along with the steam trivet to the Instant Pot. Place the pouches on top of the steam trivet. It is okay if one is on top of another.

Secure the lid with the steam vent sealed. Press "Steam" and then use the "−/+" button to adjust the time until the display reads 9 minutes.

When the timer is done, allow the pressure to natural release for 2 minutes. Quick release the remaining pressure.

Remove the lid and carefully remove the pouches. Open the parchment and eat the fish and "noodles" right out of the pouch.

TIP: This recipe can be halved to make a perfect dinner for two.

"GIMME-ALL-THE-MUSHROOMS" *Ramen*

PREP TIME: 17–19 MINUTES
COOK TIME: 35 MINUTES
SERVES 4

I am late to the ramen trend. I never lived off ramen in college. I live off it now as a poor homeowner adult who wants a quick, tasty, slurpy meal. Mushrooms, dried and fresh, are an obvious match for ramen. I love the fact that they are so hearty, yet light. Plus those little pockets and folds underneath the mushroom are perfect for absorbing all types of flavors. Not only does the pressure cooking extract all the mushroom flavor, it also allows it to infuse the noodles! Nothing about this ramen comes close to that poor college kid standard.

1 tbsp (15 ml) extra-virgin olive oil

1 tsp sesame oil

8 oz (230 g) baby bella mushrooms, sliced

1 yellow onion, diced

½ tsp minced garlic

1 dried star anise

1 dried cinnamon stick

1 dried bay leaf

½ tsp anchovy paste, optional

1 oz (28 g) dried shiitake mushrooms

¼ cup (60 ml) low-sodium soy sauce

1 tsp salt

½ tsp freshly ground black pepper

⅛ tsp crushed red pepper flakes

4 cups (950 ml) water

4 cups (950 ml) vegetable stock or low-sodium chicken stock

9 oz (258 g) packaged ramen noodles

2 Just-Right Jammy Eggs (page 159), sliced in half, for garnish

2 sliced green onions, for garnish

Sesame seeds, for garnish

Add the olive oil and sesame oil to the Instant Pot. Press "Sauté" and wait 2 minutes for the pot to heat up.

Add the baby bella mushrooms and onion to the pot. Stir and sauté until slightly golden, about 10 minutes.

Press "Cancel." Add the garlic, anise, cinnamon, bay leaf, anchovy paste (if desired) and dried shiitake to the pot. Stir to combine.

Mix in the soy sauce, salt, black pepper, red pepper flakes, water and stock. Secure the lid, leaving the vent in the closed position. Press "Soup/Broth," and then use the "−/+" button to adjust the time display to read 35 minutes.

Once the mushrooms are cooked, quick release the pressure. Remove the lid and the large shiitake mushrooms. Slice the mushrooms into bite-size pieces, and then return them to the pot.

Add in the noodles and stir to combine. Press "Sauté" and cook the noodles for 5 to 7 minutes, until tender.

Ladle the broth into bowls. Use tongs to transfer the noodles and mushrooms to the bowls. Top with the Just-Right Jammy Egg halves, sliced green onions and sesame seeds.

FRIED-EGG *Spaghetti*

This is the dish that happens when you want breakfast for dinner but don't want to give up on the noodles. It is the best of both worlds. I love that you can fry your eggs and cook your pasta all in one device. Better yet, everything gets cooked up in that wonderful bacon grease. This dish has a bit more prep because you have to partially fry the eggs and cook the bacon ahead of time. You make up for that time when the noodles are done in 6 minutes. A dinner done in much less than 30 minutes. And you get bacon on top of it. Win-win, right?

6 slices raw bacon, chopped

2 tbsp (30 g) unsalted butter

4 large eggs

1 yellow onion, finely diced

1 jarred roasted red pepper, thinly sliced

½ tsp crushed red pepper flakes

2 cloves garlic, minced

16 oz (450 g) dry spaghetti, broken in half

3½ cups (840 ml) chicken stock or water

1 tsp salt, plus more to taste

¼ tsp freshly ground black pepper, plus more to taste

½ cup (50 g) freshly grated Parmesan cheese, plus more to taste

Press "Sauté." Add the bacon to the Instant Pot and cook until crispy, about 8 minutes. Remove with a slotted spoon and transfer to a paper towel–lined plate.

Add the butter to the pot. Once the butter melts, swirl it around to combine it with the bacon grease.

Carefully crack the eggs into the Instant Pot. Cook them for 6 to 7 minutes, until the whites are just about set. Carefully remove the eggs with a large spatula and transfer them to a plate.

Press "Cancel." Mix in the onion, roasted red pepper, red pepper flakes and garlic. Use a wooden spoon to scrape off the burnt bits of bacon from the bottom of the pot.

Add the pasta, stock or water, salt and pepper to the pot. Secure the lid, leaving the vent in the closed position. Press "Pressure Cook" until the light is underneath "High Pressure." Use the "−/+" button to adjust the time until the display reads 6 minutes.

When the noodles are cooked, quick release the pressure. Remove the lid and toss the noodles with tongs to separate.

Cut the eggs into 1-inch (2.5-cm) pieces and add them back to the pot along with the bacon and Parmesan. Mix using the tongs.

Top with some more Parmesan, salt and pepper if needed.

TIP: The lazy approach to this dish would be to use leftover Just-Right Jammy Eggs (page 159) to save some time on the front end. The yolks still create a good sauce with the bacon and pasta.

CREAMY SUN-DRIED-TOMATO *Tortellini*

PREP TIME: 5 MINUTES
COOK TIME: 2 MINUTES
OR 1 HOUR 20 MINUTES
SERVES 4

Tart sun-dried tomatoes are meant to be slathered in cheese and cream, right? Tortellini cooks quickly normally, so I have included two different cooking methods for those days when you either have things to do while dinner cooks or want pasta in two minutes! Two minutes!!! You read that correctly.

1¾ cups (420 ml) vegetable stock

1 heaping tbsp (16 g) tomato paste

1 cup (110 g) julienned sun-dried tomatoes

¼ cup (40 g) diced yellow onion

¼ tsp crushed red pepper flakes

1 clove garlic, minced

1 tsp salt

¼ tsp freshly ground black pepper

½ tsp dried oregano

12 oz (340 g) uncooked cheese tortellini

⅓ cup (80 ml) heavy cream

⅓ cup (35 g) freshly grated Parmesan cheese

Fresh chopped basil, for garnish

Combine the stock, tomato paste, tomatoes, onion, red pepper flakes, garlic, salt, pepper and oregano in the Instant Pot. Mix in the tortellini.

To pressure cook, secure the lid and place the vent in the closed position. Press "Pressure Cook" until the display light is underneath "High Pressure." Use the "−/+" button to adjust the time until the display reads 2 minutes.

When the noodles are cooked, quick release the pressure. Remove the lid and mix in the cream and Parmesan. Garnish with basil.

SLOW COOKER OPTION: To slow cook, add the vegetable stock, tomato paste, sun-dried tomatoes, onion, red pepper flakes, garlic, salt, pepper, oregano and tortellini to the Instant Pot. Secure the lid and leave the steam vent open. Press "Slow Cook" until the light is underneath "Low." Use the "−/+" button to adjust the time to read 1 hour and 20 minutes. Stir in the cream and Parmesan once the pasta has finished cooking. Garnish with fresh basil.

SAUSAGE & PEPPERS *Rotini*

PREP TIME: 10 MINUTES
COOK TIME: 2 HOURS 30 MINUTES—
4 HOURS 30 MINUTES OR 6 HOURS
SERVES 4

Sausage and peppers is a guaranteed way to get my vegetable-hating husband to eat a vegetable. Throw in a little spice from crushed red pepper flakes, and you are speaking my husband's love language. The thing that makes *me* love this dish is that slow-cooker setting. And the noodles, of course. The peppers, onion and sausage cook down and make the heartiest sauce. Veggie and meat lovers unite in one dish.

1 lb (450 g) mild Italian sausage (about 5 links)

1 green bell pepper, sliced

1 orange bell pepper, sliced

1 yellow onion, sliced

2 cups (475 ml) low-sodium chicken stock or water

2½ cups (600 ml) Tomato-Garlic Sauce (page 167) or marinara sauce

¼–½ tsp crushed red pepper flakes

1 tsp fresh chopped parsley

½ tsp dried oregano

½ tsp dried thyme

½ tsp salt, plus more to taste

¼ tsp freshly ground black pepper, plus more to taste

3 cups (230 g) dry rotini noodles

Place the sausage, bell peppers and onion in the Instant Pot. Top with the stock or water and the Tomato-Garlic Sauce or marinara sauce.

Mix in the red pepper flakes, parsley, oregano, thyme, salt and pepper.

Secure the lid and leave the vent in the open position. Press the "Slow Cook" button until the display light is underneath "Low." Use the "−/+" button to adjust the time until the display reads 4 hours.

After 4 hours, remove the lid, hit "Cancel," and then stir in the noodles.

Press the "Slow Cook" button until the display light is underneath "High." Use the "−/+" button to adjust the time until the display reads 30 minutes. Secure the lid and leave the vent in the open position.

Once the timer sounds, remove the lid, remove the sausages and cut them into 1-inch (2.5-cm) pieces. Mix the sausages back into the pasta and sauce. Add more salt and pepper to taste.

TIP: This recipe can be cooked on low for up to 6 hours or on high for 2 hours. Use the "Keep Warm" setting if you won't be able to get to the sausages right when the timer sounds.

Lentil-MUSHROOM BOLOGNESE

PREP TIME: 7 MINUTES
COOK TIME: 10 HOURS
SERVES 4

A pasta sauce doesn't need meat to be awesome. Just ask my carnivorous brother and husband! Mushrooms and lentils have such a hearty, earthy feel to them that they do a really good job replacing beef in this sauce. Also, if you cook anything long enough in a ton of tomatoes and garlic, it is guaranteed to be good.

2 cups (475 ml) vegetable stock

½ cup (120 ml) water

1 (14.5-oz [411-g]) can crushed tomatoes

3 cloves garlic, grated

1 tsp salt

½ tsp freshly ground black pepper

½ tsp dried oregano

½ tsp dried thyme

¼ tsp crushed red pepper flakes

1 tsp balsamic vinegar

1 tbsp (16 g) tomato paste

1 cup (190 g) dried green lentils

½ onion, diced

2 small carrots, finely grated

6 oz (170 g) cremini mushrooms, stems removed and diced

Noodles or veggie noodles, for serving

Add the vegetable stock, water, crushed tomatoes, garlic, salt, pepper, oregano, thyme, red pepper flakes, vinegar and tomato paste to the Instant Pot. Whisk until the tomato paste is completely mixed into the liquid.

Add the lentils, onion, carrots and mushrooms, and mix them into the sauce.

Secure the lid, leaving the steam vent open. Press "Slow Cook" until the light is underneath "Low." Use the "−/+" button to adjust the time until the display reads 10 hours.

Once the lentils are tender and cooked through, remove the lid and mix everything to combine. Serve with your favorite noodles or veggie noodles.

Mixed VEGETABLE LO MEIN

PREP TIME: 10 MINUTES
COOK TIME: 7 MINUTES
SERVES 4

You ever have one of those fridge- and pantry-foraging nights? You look through your crisper drawer and in your pantry to see what kind of meal you can throw together with what you have on hand. I love those nights. It is like an episode of a crazy food game show, except you get to stay in your sweatpants at home and still end up with a winning meal. This is one of those recipes. The magic of this dish is that the sauce gets thickened when it cooks with the noodles under pressure, with no added thickening agent. Basically, clean out your veggies from the fridge and pantry, throw them in with this magic sauce and voila!

1 tsp freshly grated ginger

1 tsp chili sauce

½ tsp dried minced garlic

1 tbsp (15 ml) Worcestershire sauce

1 tbsp (15 ml) red wine vinegar

¼ cup (60 ml) low-sodium soy sauce

½ tsp salt

¼ tsp freshly ground black pepper

1½ cups (360 ml) vegetable stock

10 oz (283 g) dry spaghetti noodles, cracked in half

1 red bell pepper, thinly sliced

1 cup (110 g) fresh green beans, trimmed

2 cups (240 g) chopped bok choy

2 green onions, sliced

1 cup (30 g) fresh baby spinach

½ cup (35 g) shredded red cabbage

Hot sauce, optional

Sesame seeds, for garnish

Whisk together the ginger, chili sauce, garlic, Worcestershire, vinegar, soy sauce, salt, pepper and stock in a medium mixing bowl.

Add the noodles, bell pepper and green beans to the Instant Pot. Pour the sauce over the noodles and vegetables.

Secure the lid, with the steam vent sealed. Press "Pressure Cook" until the light is beneath "High Pressure." Use the "−/+" button until the time display reads 7 minutes.

Once the timer sounds, quick release the pressure. Remove the lid and toss the noodles with tongs.

Mix in the bok choy, green onions, spinach and cabbage.

Serve the noodles with hot sauce, if desired, and garnish with the sesame seeds.

Turkey BURGER HELPER WITH PEAS

PREP TIME: 5 MINUTES
COOK TIME: 8 MINUTES
SERVES 4

As a child, I can remember looking over a big pan full of Hamburger Helper by my mom's plate as she mixed canned peas into her helping. I always thought mixing peas into the Helper was the strangest thing. . . . Until I grew up and wasn't afraid to intermingle foods. I use ground turkey for this recipe because red meat is good in moderation in our old ages, right? This dish comes together in fifteen minutes, start to finish. Cook this up for your mom or kids so they can look at you like you're nuts when you add in even more peas than the recipe calls for.

1 tsp extra-virgin olive oil

2 tbsp (30 g) unsalted butter

½ yellow onion, finely diced

1 lb (450 g) lean ground turkey

¼ tsp garlic powder

½ tsp ground mustard

1 tsp salt, plus more to taste

¼ tsp freshly ground black pepper, plus more to taste

2 cups (475 ml) low-sodium chicken stock

2½ cups (100 g) dry no-yolk egg noodles

¾ cup (110 g) frozen peas, thawed

2 tbsp (30 g) low-fat sour cream

Press "Sauté" and add the olive oil and butter to the Instant Pot.

Once the butter melts, add the onion, turkey, garlic powder, ground mustard, salt and pepper. Sauté for 5 minutes, breaking apart the turkey with a wooden spoon.

After 5 minutes, press "Cancel." Mix in the chicken stock.

Add the noodles to the pot. Secure the lid, placing the steam vent in the closed position. Press "Pressure Cook" until the display light is underneath "High Pressure." Use the "−/+" button until the time display reads 8 minutes.

Once the noodles are cooked, quick release the steam. Mix in the peas and sour cream and add more salt and pepper to taste.

SOUP'D-UP SOUPS & CHILIS

Clearly there would be an entire section dedicated to soup and chili in an Instant Pot cookbook. Come wintertime, they are the main reason that my Instant Pot lives on my countertop . . . aside from my laziness. But that laziness often leads me to throw a bunch of stuff into the Instant Pot and call it dinner, too, so you can't hate on my lazy streak too much.

For many of the soup and chili recipes in this book, I start with a classic that I love. I then turn it on its head and give it a new spin. Take, for example, chicken tortilla soup. In my head, it pairs well with a good Mexican beer, so the next obvious thought is, why not put the two together? That is how Drunken Chicken Tortilla Soup (page 92) came to be. You're welcome.

These soups and chilis are easy but also filling. If you know that person who demands a salad or sandwich with their soup, these recipes will be enough to quiet them down so they don't demand any extra food prep from your poor, tired hands.

I especially love that the soup and chili recipes can be made in different ways using the slow cooker or pressure cooker function. It's important to have the option to have dinner in an instant or when you get home from a long day of work. Soup and chili on demand for all occasions! Can't beat it.

DRUNKEN CHICKEN TORTILLA *Soup*

PREP TIME: 10 MINUTES
COOK TIME: 6–12 HOURS
SERVES 4–6

I love a good Mexican beer with a little wedge of lime nestled down in it. There is nothing better than kicking back on a hot summer day with a Mexican beer and lime. When winter rolls around and all you want is that summer beer with lime, reach for this soup instead. You still get all that Mexican beer with lots of lime flavor and get to warm up on a cold day. Truth be told, I even make this during the summer because there is never a wrong time for chicken tortilla soup.

FOR THE SOUP

16 oz (475 ml) Mexican beer

Juice from 1 lime

1 (19-oz [538-g]) can red enchilada sauce

1 (14.5-oz [411-g]) can fire-roasted diced tomatoes

1 (4-oz [113-g]) can mild green chilies

1 (29-oz [822-g]) can white hominy, drained and rinsed

2 cloves garlic, minced

1 small yellow onion, diced

1 tsp salt

¼ tsp freshly ground black pepper

1 tsp ground cumin

1 tbsp (8 g) chili powder

½ tsp dried oregano

2 large boneless, skinless chicken breasts

FOR GARNISH

Sour cream

Tortilla strips or chips

Shredded Mexican-blend cheese

Fresh chopped cilantro

Add the beer, lime juice, enchilada sauce, tomatoes, chilies, hominy, garlic, onion, salt, pepper, cumin, chili powder and oregano to the Instant Pot. Mix to combine.

Add the chicken breasts to the soup mixture.

Secure the lid, leaving the vent open. Press "Slow Cook" until the light is beneath "Low." Use the "−/+" button to adjust the time to read 12 hours. If you are cooking on "High," adjust the time to read 6 hours.

Remove the lid and transfer the chicken breasts to a plate. Use two forks to shred the chicken, and then return it to the pot. Mix to combine.

Serve the soup topped with the sour cream, tortilla strips, Mexican cheese and fresh cilantro.

SWEET & SOUR POT STICKER *Soup*

I have rediscovered my love of Asian takeout in my old age. It's sad, but my order is never that complicated, and it always includes some kind of sweet-and-sour chicken or pork. But as much as I love takeout, you can't beat home cooking because you have control over everything going into your food. I know this ingredients list is long, but did you see the cook time? Feel free to add or take away any vegetables to turn this dish into a truly customized, soul-warming soup.

¼ cup (60 ml) fish sauce

¼ cup (80 g) apricot preserves

1 tbsp (15 ml) pineapple juice

2 tbsp (30 ml) apple cider vinegar

1 tsp sriracha sauce

1 tsp grated garlic

1 tbsp (15 ml) ponzu sauce

1 tsp freshly grated ginger

⅓ cup (80 ml) low-sodium soy sauce

32 oz (950 ml) vegetable or low-sodium chicken stock

2 cups (475 ml) water

1 tsp salt

½ tsp freshly ground black pepper

1 small onion, cut into half-moons

1 yellow bell pepper, thinly sliced

1 cup (130 g) sugar snap peas, cut in half lengthwise

1 cup (150 g) carrot matchsticks

16 oz (450 g) frozen pork pot stickers, thawed

3 medium baby bok choy, sliced

3 green onions, chopped

Shredded red cabbage

Soy sauce, for topping

Hot sauce, for topping

Add the fish sauce, apricot preserves, pineapple juice, vinegar, sriracha, garlic, ponzu, ginger, soy sauce, stock, water, salt and pepper to the Instant Pot. Whisk to combine.

Add the onion, bell pepper, snap peas and carrot to the broth.

Secure the lid with the steam vent closed. Press "Pressure Cook" until the light is next to "High Pressure." Use the "−/+" button to adjust the time until the display reads 15 minutes.

When the timer sounds, quick release the steam. Mix in the pot stickers, bok choy, green onions and cabbage.

Cover with the lid. Press "Keep Warm." Once the time display reads 9 minutes, remove the lid and check that the pot stickers are heated through.

Ladle out servings of the soup and top them with soy sauce and hot sauce.

TIP: You can use whatever frozen pot stickers you would like for this soup.

SAUERKRAUT *Soup*

PREP TIME: 15 MINUTES
COOK TIME: 4–8 HOURS
OR 15 MINUTES
SERVES 4–6

This is a dish that I reach for over chicken noodle soup because it is waaaay more comforting to me. My mom is Polish. My grandfather was Polish. The smells and tastes of this soup draw on all the memories in my life that make me feel loved. It isn't pretty, yet it provides so many flavors. The balance of the saltiness from the meats with the tart sauerkraut is out of this world. When I was creating this book, this was one of the dishes I hoarded for myself. Sorry, I'm not sorry. I promise to make another batch and share the next time. Maybe.

3 strips raw bacon, diced

1 small yellow onion, diced

2 russet potatoes, diced

7 oz (202 g) smoked Polish sausage, diced

1 oz (28 g) dried mushroom medley, chopped

1 (24-oz [680-g]) jar sauerkraut, drained (I like Frank's Sauerkraut)

2 dried bay leaves

¼ tsp ground fennel seeds

½ tsp salt, plus more to taste

½ tsp freshly ground black pepper, plus more to taste

½ tsp dried thyme

3 cups (700 ml) water

4 cups (950 ml) low-sodium chicken stock

Fresh chopped parsley, for garnish

Add the bacon to the Instant Pot. Press "Sauté," and cook the bacon until crispy, 7 to 10 minutes.

Remove the bacon with a slotted spoon and transfer it to a paper towel–lined plate. Wipe out three-quarters of the bacon grease with a paper towel.

Add the onion, potatoes and sausage. Sauté 5 to 7 minutes, until slightly crispy.

Mix in the mushrooms and sauerkraut, deglazing the pot.

Press "Cancel." Mix in the bay leaves, fennel, salt, pepper and thyme.

Add the water and stock.

Secure the lid, leaving the vent open. Press "Slow Cook" until the light is under "Low." Use the "–/+" button to adjust the time display to read 8 hours. Or cook on "High" and adjust the time display to read 4 hours.

Remove the lid, discard the bay leaves and adjust the salt and pepper to taste. Ladle out the soup into bowls. Garnish with the parsley.

PRESSURE COOKER OPTION: After sautéing the bacon and draining some of the fat, sauté the sausage and onion for 5 minutes. Mix in the onions, potatoes, mushrooms, sauerkraut, bay leaves, fennel, salt, pepper, thyme, water and stock. Secure the lid, press "Pressure Cook" and make sure the light is beneath "High Pressure." Use the "–/+" button to adjust the time until the display reads 15 minutes. When the timer sounds, quick release the pressure, remove the lid, discard the bay leaves and adjust the salt and pepper to taste. Garnish with the parsley.

CHORIZO & CAULIFLOWER RICE *Chili*

PREP TIME: 10 MINUTES
COOK TIME: 10 MINUTES
SERVES 4-6

I add beans to most things. That is common knowledge. Some people, shockingly, do not like beans in everything, even when it comes to chili. Some people, maybe the same people, also don't like chili served over rice. You know what I say to that? Hide the beans and rice in the chili! Ha! Mix a little bit of refried beans and cauliflower "rice" into this smoky and spicy chili, and nobody is the wiser. This is a super-thick chili that comes together in less than 30 minutes.

1 tbsp (15 ml) extra-virgin olive oil

1 lb (450 g) ground pork chorizo

½ yellow onion, diced

1 tbsp (10 g) diced jalapeño

¼ cup (65 g) tomato paste

1 tbsp (8 g) chili powder

1 tsp salt

¼ tsp freshly ground black pepper

1 tsp ground cumin

½ tsp dried oregano

1-2 tsp (5-10 ml) liquid from a can of chipotles in adobo sauce

1 (10-oz [283-g]) can fire-roasted diced tomatoes with green chilies

2 cups (475 ml) low-sodium chicken stock

¾ cup (180 g) canned refried beans or Salsa-Style Refried Black Beans with Bacon (page 134)

2 cups (300 g) frozen riced cauliflower

OPTIONAL TOPPINGS

Shredded cheese

Sour cream

Not-Another-Restaurant Salsa (page 163)

Press "Sauté" and add the olive oil to the Instant Pot. Wait 1 minute, then add the chorizo, onion and jalapeño. Sauté for 5 minutes, using a wooden spoon to break up the chorizo.

Add the tomato paste, chili powder, salt, pepper, cumin, oregano and adobo liquid. Mix to combine. Sauté for 1 minute.

Press "Cancel." Mix in the tomatoes, stock and beans.

Secure the lid with the steam vent sealed. Press "Pressure Cook" and ensure the light is on beneath "High Pressure." Use the "−/+" button to adjust the time until the display reads 10 minutes.

Once the timer sounds, quick release the pressure. Press "Keep Warm" and remove the lid. Mix in the cauliflower rice.

Let the rice sit in the pot for 2 to 4 minutes until tender.

Press "Cancel" and then serve the chili with whichever toppings you prefer, such as shredded cheese, sour cream and a spoonful of Not-Another-Restaurant Salsa (page 163).

Creamy GARLIC, BACON, POTATO & KALE SOUP

PREP TIME: 15 MINUTES
COOK TIME: 7 MINUTES
SERVES 4–6

Did you guys jump on the kale train? I remember trying kale chips when they first came on the scene. As the crispy kale disintegrated on my tongue, I thought, nope, no way is this a chip. I get how good it is for you, though. I'm all for using it in salads and soups. A little kick of an almost broccoli-like healthfulness in the background. With something that super healthy, we need bacon to even things out. Mix in a good measure of cream cheese at the end, because kale tastes even better smothered in a creamy soup.

6 slices raw bacon, chopped

1 yellow onion, diced

1 carrot, peeled and diced

1 celery stalk, diced

3 large russet potatoes, peeled and cut into ½-inch (1-cm) cubes

5 cloves garlic, peeled and grated

1 tsp salt, plus more to taste

½ tsp freshly ground black pepper, plus more to taste

½ tsp ground mustard

24 oz (700 ml) low-sodium chicken stock

2 cups (475 ml) whole milk

2 tbsp (15 g) cornstarch

6 cups (400 g) chopped kale

3 oz (85 g) cream cheese, cubed

Press "Sauté" and add the bacon to the Instant Pot. Sauté until crisp, 5 to 7 minutes. Remove it with a slotted spoon and transfer it to a plate lined with a paper towel.

Add the onion, carrot, celery and potatoes. Sauté for 5 minutes, mixing intermittently.

Press "Cancel." Mix in the garlic, salt, pepper and ground mustard, and sauté for 1 minute.

Pour in the chicken stock.

Secure the lid and move the vent to the closed position. Press "Pressure Cook" until the light is underneath "High Pressure." Use the "−/+" button until the display reads 7 minutes.

Once the timer sounds, natural release the pressure for 5 minutes. Quick release the remaining steam.

Whisk together the milk and cornstarch in a small bowl. Remove the lid from the Instant Pot. Add the milk–cornstarch slurry to the pot and mix to combine.

Press "Sauté" and add the kale and cream cheese. Stir until the cream cheese melts and the soup thickens.

Press "Cancel." Adjust the salt and pepper to taste.

COLD-FIGHTING CHICKEN NOODLE *Soup*

PREP TIME: 15 MINUTES
COOK TIME: 8 HOURS
30 MINUTES
SERVES 4-6

In my old age, I have been finding that the stuff that kicks my cold the quickest is all natural. Fresh ginger, lemon juice, hot water, cayenne pepper, turmeric and garlic are all I need to get that cold outta here. I took my mom's version of homemade chicken noodle soup and went to town on it with my arsenal of home remedies to make this slow-cooked soup. Make a big batch and freeze it so the next time a cold hits, you don't have to spend a fortune at the drugstore.

2 cups (475 ml) low-sodium chicken stock

3 cups (700 ml) water

2 large boneless, skinless chicken breasts

½ yellow onion, diced

3 celery stalks, chopped

3 carrots, peeled and chopped

Zest and juice of 1 lemon

1 tbsp (15 g) salt, plus more to taste

¼–½ tsp cayenne pepper, to preference, plus more to taste

½ tsp freshly ground black pepper, plus more to taste

1 tbsp (7 g) ground turmeric

1 tbsp (6 g) freshly grated ginger

2 cloves garlic, grated

1 dried bay leaf

2 fresh thyme sprigs

2 cups (76 g) dry no-yolk egg noodles

Add the stock, water, chicken, onion, celery, carrots, lemon zest, lemon juice, salt, cayenne, pepper, turmeric, ginger, garlic, bay leaf and thyme to the Instant Pot. Mix to combine.

Seal the lid with the steam vent to open. Press the "Slow Cook" button until the display light is under "Less." Press the "–/+" button until the time display reads 8 hours.

After 8 hours, remove the lid and transfer the chicken breasts to a plate. Shred the chicken using two forks. Add the shredded chicken back to the pot along with the noodles.

Set the Instant Pot to "Slow Cook" on "Less" for another 25 to 30 minutes, until the noodles are al dente.

Remove the bay leaf and thyme sprigs. Add more salt, pepper or cayenne to taste.

Butternut Squash & PUMPKIN SOUP

PREP TIME: 5 MINUTES
COOK TIME: 20 MINUTES
SERVES 4-6

I am going to offend some people with the following statement, but I will say it anyway: This is my girly soup. It's like the pumpkin spice latte of the soup world. All the guys in my life turn their noses up at this, whereas all the ladies love it. There is something about the complexity of the sweet and savory combo of smooth and creamy butternut squash and pumpkin that women just understand and appreciate better than men. That's okay guys; take a pass. More for us.

12 oz (340 g) frozen cubed butternut squash

1 cup (245 g) pumpkin puree

1 tomato, chopped

1 yellow onion, chopped

¼ tsp ground nutmeg

¼ tsp ground cinnamon

½ tsp chili powder

½ tsp smoked paprika

1½ cups (360 ml) low-sodium chicken or vegetable stock

2 cloves garlic, peeled and smashed

½ tsp salt, plus more to taste

¼ tsp freshly ground black pepper, plus more to taste

¼ cup (60 ml) heavy whipping cream

1 cup (30 g) croutons, for topping

Add the butternut squash, pumpkin puree, tomato, onion, nutmeg, cinnamon, chili powder, paprika, stock, garlic, salt and pepper to the Instant Pot. Stir to combine.

Secure the lid with the steam vent closed. Press "Pressure Cook" until the display light is beneath "High Pressure." Use the "−/+" button to adjust the time until the display reads 20 minutes.

Once the timer is done, quick release the steam.

Remove the lid. Add in the heavy cream. Use an immersion blender to puree the soup until smooth. Or, let the soup cool, and then transfer the mixture to a blender and puree.

Add more salt and pepper to taste. Garnish with some croutons before serving.

TIP: Using frozen butternut squash is a major time-saver. If you use fresh butternut squash, just increase the cooking time by 10 minutes.

CHILI RELLENO *Soup*

With so many amazing tacos and meats to choose from at your favorite Mexican restaurant, why go for chili relleno? Um, duh, cheese! Chili Relleno Soup is my take on the classic dish, and the slow-cooker feature on the Instant Pot allows the cheese to stay gooey and coat all the smoky poblano peppers perfectly. While you're eating this soup, you'll still get all those glorious cheese pulls for which chili relleno is famous. You won't even find yourself missing that fried coating on the peppers one bit.

2 tbsp (30 ml) olive oil

1 tbsp (15 g) unsalted butter

3 poblano peppers, seeded and diced

1 yellow onion, diced

1 jalapeño, seeded and diced

1 tsp salt, plus more to taste

3 cloves garlic, grated

½ tsp freshly ground black pepper, plus more to taste

½ tsp ground cumin

¼ tsp chili powder

¼ tsp smoked paprika

⅓ cup (40 g) all-purpose flour

1¾ cups (420 ml) low-sodium chicken stock

1 (14.5-oz [411-g]) can fire-roasted diced tomatoes, rinsed and drained

1¾ cups (420 ml) heavy cream

2 cups (226 g) shredded pepper jack cheese, plus more for topping

2 tbsp (2 g) fresh chopped cilantro

Press "Sauté." Add the olive oil and butter to the Instant Pot.

Once the butter melts, add the poblano peppers, onion and jalapeño. Sauté for 6 minutes.

Mix in the salt, garlic, pepper, cumin, chili powder, paprika and flour.

Whisk in the stock, tomatoes and heavy cream.

Secure the lid and leave the steam vent open. Press "Slow Cook" until the display light is under "High." Use the "−/+" button until the time display reads 3 hours.

Once the soup is cooked, press "Keep Warm," and then add in the cheese. Mix until the cheese is melted and combined.

Add more salt and pepper to taste. Mix in the cilantro, reserving a little for garnish.

Posole VERDE WITH SHRIMP

Have you ever been to a really good Mexican restaurant and decided to get not only the second basket of free chips and salsa, but also the posole and an entrée of tacos? This has happened to me more than I would like to admit. Posole is a thick, fire-roasted tomato- or tomatillo-based soup thicker than a soup but not quite a chili. Normally, this soup takes a while to cook and develop flavors, but under pressure you get those results in no time. You could even eat another serving of chips and salsa while you cook this at home, if you really want to set the scene.

4 tomatillos, husks removed and quartered

1 yellow onion, roughly chopped

2 pasilla peppers, seeds and stem removed, roughly chopped

1 jalapeño pepper, seeds and stem removed, chopped

2 cloves garlic, peeled and smashed

8 oz (240 ml) Mexican beer

Juice of 1 lime

1 (7-oz [202-g]) can mild green chilies

3 cups (700 ml) low-sodium chicken stock

1 tbsp (15 ml) Spicy Zhoug Sauce (page 164)

1 tsp salt, plus more to taste

1 lb (450 g) deveined, tail-on shrimp

½ cup (8 g) fresh cilantro leaves

Freshly ground black pepper, to taste

Grilled corn, for topping

Shredded green or red cabbage, for topping

Sliced radishes, for topping

Lime wedges, for serving

Press "Sauté," and then add the tomatillos, onion, pasilla peppers and jalapeño to the pot. Sear for about 7 minutes, until the edges get dark brown.

Press "Cancel." Add the garlic and mix to combine. Deglaze the pot with the beer. Add the lime juice and green chilies. Mix to combine, scraping up any burnt bits from the bottom of the pot.

Mix in the chicken stock, Spicy Zhoug Sauce and salt.

Secure the lid with the steam vent sealed. Press "Pressure Cook" until the light is underneath "High Pressure," and use the "−/+" button to adjust the time until the display reads 15 minutes.

Once the timer sounds, quick release the pressure. Remove the lid and add the shrimp. Secure the lid. Let the shrimp cook in the liquid for 5 to 7 minutes, until opaque.

Remove the lid and transfer the shrimp to a plate.

Add the cilantro, and stir to combine. Use an immersion blender to puree the soup until it's smooth. Add more salt or pepper to taste.

Add the shrimp back to the soup. Ladle out servings of the soup, and top each with corn, shredded cabbage, radishes and a wedge of lime.

HEARTY CHICKEN & VEGETABLE *Stew*

PREP TIME: 10 MINUTES
COOK TIME: 30 MINUTES
SERVES 4–6

Like most home cooks, I always have chicken on hand, along with celery, carrots, potatoes and onions. Those vegetables are such a great base for all the classic comfort foods, this stew included. It's inspired by a cold-weather household favorite my mom made for us growing up. My brothers and I still request it to this day. The only difference is her version takes three hours and mine takes much less than one hour. That is why she usually gripes when we ask her to make it. Now I can fill the stew void in the family any time I want!

1 lb (450 g) boneless, skinless chicken breasts, cut into 1-inch (2.5-cm) cubes

2 tbsp (15 g) cornstarch

1 tsp salt

½ tsp freshly ground black pepper

1 (10.75-oz [305-g]) can condensed tomato soup

2 cups (475 ml) low-sodium chicken stock

1 large tomato, chopped

2 russet potatoes, chopped

1 yellow onion, chopped

2 celery stalks, chopped

2 carrots, peeled and chopped

½ lb (230 g) fresh green beans, trimmed

3 fresh thyme sprigs

Sliced rye bread or a French baguette, for serving

Toss the chicken, cornstarch, salt and pepper together in a mixing bowl.

Add the condensed soup, stock and chopped tomato to the Instant Pot. Mix to combine.

Add the potatoes, onion, celery, carrots, green beans and chicken to the pot. Top with the thyme sprigs. Mix to submerge as many of the vegetables as possible in the liquid.

Secure the lid, with the vent in the sealed position. Press "Meat/Stew," and then use the "–/+" button to adjust the time until the display reads 30 minutes.

Once the soup is done cooking, quick release the pressure. Remove the lid and discard the thyme stems. Serve the stew with a nice piece of crusty bread.

CAN'T-BEAT-IT TURKEY & BACON *Chili*

PREP TIME: 18–23 MINUTES
COOK TIME: 20 MINUTES
SERVES 4–6

In all my years of blogging, this is my all-time favorite chili recipe. That means a lot because some of my chili recipes have won local cook-offs for my friends. The combination of seasonings and the use of tomato paste under pressure add so much flavor to plain old ground turkey. Bacon adds the fat that can sometimes be lacking in ground turkey dishes.

5 raw bacon slices, chopped

1 yellow onion, diced

1 red or yellow bell pepper, diced

3 cloves garlic, grated

1½ lbs (680 g) lean ground turkey

2 tbsp (15 g) chili powder

1 tsp salt, plus more to taste

½ tsp freshly ground black pepper, plus more to taste

1 tsp dried oregano

1 tsp ground cumin

1 tsp smoked paprika

6 oz (170 g) tomato paste

1 tbsp (15 ml) Worcestershire sauce

1 (10-oz [283-g]) can diced tomatoes with green chilies

1 (15-oz [425-g]) can pinto beans, drained and rinsed

1 (15.5-oz [439-g]) can black beans, drained and rinsed

1 (15-oz [425-g]) can red kidney beans, drained and rinsed

2½ cups (600 ml) low-sodium chicken stock

Set your Instant Pot to "Sauté." Add the bacon. Stir and cook until crispy, about 7 minutes. Remove it with a slotted spoon and set it off to the side on a paper towel–lined plate. Drain off all the grease except for ½ teaspoon.

Add the onion, bell pepper and garlic. Sauté for 1 minute.

Add the turkey along with the chili powder, salt, pepper, oregano, cumin and paprika. Use a wooden spoon to break the turkey into small pieces, making sure the seasoning is evenly distributed. Cook until the turkey is browned, 10 to 15 minutes.

Add the tomato paste, Worcestershire and canned tomatoes. Stir to combine.

Add the pinto beans, black beans, kidney beans and stock. Stir to combine.

Secure the lid with the steam vent sealed. Press "Pressure Cook" until the light is underneath "High Pressure." Use the "–/+" button to adjust the time until the display reads 20 minutes.

When the chili is done cooking, quick release the pressure. Remove the lid and stir the chili. Add more salt and pepper to taste.

Eggplant & TOMATO SOUP

What are winter and fall without tomato soup? My version is a little different. I love to add meaty and mild eggplant to thicken up the soup and to add another dimension of flavor. Cooking this soup slowly really allows the flavors to develop. I think this version of tomato soup will become your new cold weather go-to.

2 tbsp (30 ml) extra-virgin olive oil

1 large eggplant, cubed

1 yellow onion, chopped

1 tsp salt

½ tsp freshly ground black pepper

1 clove garlic, grated

2 tbsp (30 ml) dry cooking sherry

1 tsp lemon juice

1 (28-oz [794-g]) can whole peeled tomatoes

12 oz (355 ml) water

1 cup (240 ml) low-sodium chicken or vegetable stock

1 fresh thyme sprig

1 fresh rosemary sprig

4 basil leaves

Pinch of fresh parsley, for garnish

Add the olive oil to the Instant Pot. Press "Sauté." Once the olive oil starts to shimmer, add the eggplant and onion. Sauté for about 10 minutes, stirring regularly.

Season with the salt and pepper. Mix to combine. Add in the garlic and stir.

Press "Cancel." Pour in the sherry and lemon juice to deglaze the pot. Mix to combine.

Mix in the tomatoes, water, stock, thyme, rosemary and basil.

Secure the lid, leaving the steam vent open. Press "Slow Cook" until the light is beneath "Less." Use the "−/+" button to adjust the time until the display reads 6 hours.

After 6 hours, remove the lid and remove the thyme and rosemary stems, leaving the leaves behind.

Use an immersion blender to puree the soup until smooth. Or wait for the soup to cool, and puree it in a blender until smooth.

Serve with fresh parsley on top alongside a good grilled cheese sandwich.

BEANS, VEGETABLES & GRAINS in a SNAP

When you think of the Instant Pot and all the things you could be cooking with it, I doubt your mind goes to vegetables. But the truth is that the steam setting is key to the creation of the best vegetables, such as potatoes, asparagus, green beans and acorn squash.

The Instant Pot is also the main reason I switched over to using dry beans. A bag of dry beans is a dollar or two, and it yields so much. That means one less thing to remember at the grocery store. It is so nice to just reach into your freezer as opposed to rage searching through all the random things in your pantry just to realize you forgot the beans (not that I do that or anything).

None of the bean recipes in this book require soaking the beans overnight. That was also my main qualm with dry beans. If you forget to soak the beans for stovetop cooking, no worries. I've got you covered.

Now that I have convinced you to cook all the veggies in your Instant Pot, let's move on to the no-brainer: rice and grains.

I always mess up stovetop rice and grains. I measure the water, I set the timer and I do all the right things. Every time I end up with too much water left over or gummy, overcooked rice. Honestly, this is a real disease. I think I inherited it from my mom. I don't even try anymore. I bust out the Instant Pot and it seriously takes care of the rest. Perfect every single time.

Given the Instant Pot's versatility and that vegetables and grains are basically blank canvases for any flavor you want, you'll for sure be steaming up beans and vegetables and savoring forkfuls of fluffy rice for years to come!

ROASTED VEGETABLE
Mediterranean RICE

PREP TIME: 7 MINUTES
COOK TIME: 20 MINUTES
SERVES 4–6

The first time I made a version of this dish, it was served alongside some spicy salmon. Why doesn't this dish include salmon? Well, because all anybody kept talking about was the rice. Steamed rice with my favorite zhoug sauce serves as the perfect bed for artichoke hearts, roasted red pepper and sun-dried tomatoes. You still get all that roasted vegetable flavor from the zhoug and red peppers without using your oven. You won't even be asking for a main dish with this on the table!

1¼ cups (300 ml) water or low-sodium chicken stock

1 cup (190 g) brown rice

¾ cup (85 g) jarred sun-dried tomatoes, drained

1 jarred roasted red pepper, drained and chopped

6 oz (170 g) frozen artichoke hearts, thawed

2 tbsp (30 ml) Spicy Zhoug Sauce (page 164)

½ tsp salt, plus more to taste

½ cup (75 g) diced red onion

1 tbsp (5 g) fresh chopped parsley

Add the water or stock, rice, tomatoes, red pepper, artichoke hearts, Spicy Zhoug Sauce and salt to the Instant Pot. Mix to combine.

Secure the lid, leaving the vent in the closed position. Press "Pressure Cook" until the display light is beneath "High Pressure." Use the "−/+" button until the time display reads 20 minutes.

Once the timer sounds, natural release the steam for 10 minutes. Quick release any remaining steam.

Remove the lid and fluff the rice with a fork. Add more salt to taste.

Mix in the red onion and parsley before serving.

THE BEST *Elote*

PREP TIME: 10 MINUTES
COOK TIME: 5 MINUTES
SERVES 4

I know titling something "the best" is a bold claim to make. I am prepared to back it up 100 percent. It begins with the perfectly steamed tender corn, which makes the ideal base. Then the easiest garlic-cream sauce. Last, rolling the cobs in the sauce and topping them with cheese, chili-lime seasoning and cilantro. All the toppings stick to the sauce perfectly. Every kernel gets coated in flavor. After your first bite, you'll call it the best too!

1 cup (240 ml) water

4 ears of corn, husks on, with ends trimmed to fit the Instant Pot

1 tbsp (15 g) unsalted butter

¼ cup (60 ml) heavy cream

Pinch of salt

Pinch of freshly ground black pepper

¼ tsp minced garlic

1 tbsp (12 g) mayonnaise

1 tbsp (15 g) sour cream

¼ cup (30 g) queso fresco crumbles

1 tbsp (13 g) chili-lime seasoning

1 tbsp (1 g) fresh chopped cilantro

1 tsp lime juice

Add the water and steam trivet to the Instant Pot. Arrange the corn on top of the trivet.

Secure the lid with the steam vent in the sealed position. Press "Steam," and then use the "−/+" button to adjust the time to read 5 minutes.

Once the corn is steamed, quick release the pressure. Use tongs to transfer the corn to a plate. Carefully peel back the husks to use as a handle for the corn.

Press "Keep Warm" and add the butter, cream, salt, pepper and garlic to the pot. Whisk to combine. Once the timer display reads 1 minute, hit "Cancel."

Whisk in the mayonnaise and sour cream.

Pour the sauce into a shallow, rimmed plate. Roll each corn cob in the sauce. Sprinkle the top of each cob with the queso fresco, chili-lime seasoning, cilantro and lime juice.

Decadent CAULIFLOWER & POTATO MASH

PREP TIME: 7 MINUTES
COOK TIME: 10 MINUTES
SERVES 4–6

My mom makes the best mashed potatoes. I will argue with you to the death on this matter. I always try to re-create her recipe. Spoiler alert: It never tastes the same. I basically gave up after all these years. I decided to go my own way and make an easier and more balanced version of mashed potatoes. I kept the same hard-hitting ingredients she uses: heavy cream, butter, cream cheese and sour cream. Then I boosted the healthfulness with some cauliflower, because balance. I like to think my recipe is better because it is done all in one pot and takes way less time. Sorry, Mom.

1 cup (240 ml) water

5 russet potatoes, peeled and halved

½ head cauliflower

½ cup (120 ml) heavy whipping cream

¼ cup (60 g) unsalted butter

1 tsp salt, plus more to taste

½ tsp freshly ground black pepper

4 tbsp (60 g) cream cheese, room temperature

2 tbsp (30 g) sour cream

1 tbsp (3 g) chopped chives, for garnish

Add the water along with the steam trivet to the Instant Pot. Place the potatoes and cauliflower on top of the trivet.

Secure the lid with the steam vent sealed. Press "Steam," and then use the "–/+" button to adjust the time until the display reads 10 minutes.

Once the potatoes and cauliflower are steamed, quick release the pressure. Carefully remove the trivet and transfer the potatoes and cauliflower to a plate. Discard the water, and place the insert back into the Instant Pot.

Add the potatoes and cauliflower back into the pot along with the heavy cream, butter, salt, pepper, cream cheese and sour cream. Press "Keep Warm."

Use a potato masher to mash the potatoes and cauliflower until smooth. You can also use an immersion blender if you prefer very smooth potatoes.

Add more salt to taste. Serve the potatoes on a large platter garnished with chopped chives.

CHEESY BROCCOLI-LOADED *Hasselback* POTATOES

PREP TIME: 10 MINUTES
COOK TIME: 15 MINUTES
SERVES 4

Who doesn't love a good baked potato? I usually slather mine with butter, salt, pepper, sour cream and a few good dashes of hot sauce. When I do that, I am usually eating the potato as a side. However, sometimes I want more out of my potato. I hate having the oven on for a long time, though. It's like, not only am I baking potatoes, I am baking my house too. I make these cheesy broccoli-loaded potatoes either one at a time for me or a few at a time for weekly meal prep. It's a time-saving way to spice up your usual baked potato—plus, you don't heat your entire house.

4 russet potatoes

4 tbsp (60 g) cold unsalted butter

Salt, to taste

Freshly ground black pepper, to taste

1 cup (240 ml) water

1 cup (160 g) frozen broccoli, thawed and chopped

¾ cup (85 g) shredded cheddar cheese

¼ cup (22 g) shredded Parmesan cheese

Make about ten slices on the top of each potato, slicing three-quarters of the way through the potato and leaving about ¼ inch (6 mm) between each cut.

Thinly slice the butter. Place a slice in every other slit in the potatoes. Sprinkle a little salt and pepper on top of each potato.

Add the water and steamer trivet to the Instant Pot. Place the potatoes on the trivet. Secure the lid and place the vent in the closed position.

Press "Pressure Cook" until the light is underneath "High Pressure." Use the "−/+" button until the time display reads 12 minutes.

Once the potatoes are done, quick release the steam. Remove the lid. Carefully remove the trivet with the potatoes. Stuff two to three broccoli florets and about 1 teaspoon of cheddar and Parmesan down into each slit. Sprinkle the cheese on top of the potatoes. Place the trivet with the potatoes back into the Instant Pot.

Secure the lid and leave the vent in the open position. Press the "Keep Warm" button. Let the potatoes sit in the pot for 3 minutes, until the cheese melts.

Carefully remove the potatoes and serve with a dash of salt and pepper.

CHILI-LIME *Asparagus*

Are you familiar with Tajin? It is a chili, lime and salt seasoning I came across in 2011 on my honeymoon in Mexico. Naturally, it was on a cocktail. You may be familiar with this reddish seasoning from elote, or Mexican street corn. Well, I caught on to that salty, spicy, secret seasoning and started adding it to more and more food in place of salt. It adds so much to this side, which requires just a quick steam in the Instant Pot to bring everything together.

1 tbsp (15 ml) extra-virgin olive oil

½ cup (75 g) diced red bell pepper

1 lb (450 g) fresh asparagus, trimmed

¼ tsp ground cumin

¼ tsp freshly ground black pepper

½ tsp chili-lime seasoning

Juice of 1 lime

Fresh chopped cilantro, for garnish

1 radish, diced, for garnish

Sliced jalapeños, optional, for garnish

Press the "Sauté" button on the Instant Pot. Add the olive oil and bell pepper. Mix and sauté for 4 minutes. Press "Cancel."

Mix in the asparagus, cumin, pepper, chili-lime seasoning and lime juice.

Secure the lid and place the vent in the closed position. Press the "Steam" button. Use the "–/+" button to adjust the time until the display reads 3 minutes.

Once the timer sounds, quick release the steam.

Transfer the asparagus and peppers to a serving dish using tongs. Pour any liquid from the pot over the asparagus. Top it with the cilantro, radish and jalapeño, if using.

MAPLE-CAYENNE
Hasselback
SWEET POTATOES

PREP TIME: 10 MINUTES
COOK TIME: 17 MINUTES
SERVES 4

I can handle spicy. Most of the time. Will I go out of my way to make or order something with the word *diablo* in the description? Nope. So trust me when I say this recipe title may contain the word *cayenne* but that even you low-spice-tolerance folks will be able to handle this. The smooth, creamy sweet potato along with the maple syrup balance out the spice. Also, just to reiterate, if you couldn't already tell, the Instant Pot is my favorite way to cook perfect potatoes every single time. Perfect potato plus perfect spice balance equals, well, perfection!

4 small or medium sweet potatoes

1 tbsp (15 ml) maple syrup

¼ tsp cayenne pepper

4 tbsp (60 g) unsalted butter

Pinch of salt, plus more to taste

1 cup (240 ml) water

Freshly ground black pepper, to taste

Make cuts about ¼ inch (6 mm) apart and about three-quarters of the way down into each sweet potato.

Combine the maple syrup, cayenne, butter and salt in a small mixing bowl.

Add the water and the steam trivet to the Instant Pot. Place the sweet potatoes on the trivet.

Spread the butter mixture evenly on each sweet potato, reserving half of the mixture.

Secure the lid and close the steam vent. Press "Pressure Cook" until the light is underneath "High Pressure" and use the "−/+" button until the time display reads 17 minutes.

Natural release the pressure for 10 minutes. When the potatoes are cooked, quick release the remaining pressure.

Carefully transfer the sweet potatoes to a serving plate. Spread the remaining cayenne–maple butter on top of each sweet potato.

Finish each potato with a sprinkle of salt and pepper.

GARLIC-LOADED FRESH CREAMED *Spinach*

PREP TIME: 5 MINUTES
COOK TIME: 7 MINUTES
SERVES 4–6

This dish would probably be nightmare material for a child. But then you grow up and realize your body needs green things, and hey, they don't taste that bad after all! Then you start asking yourself, what did that childhood version of me really know about good food anyway? So, you steam all the fresh spinach in your Instant Pot and then add all the garlic, cream and cheese, because you're an adult and you can make vegetables that actually taste good and still slightly benefit you!

2 tbsp (30 ml) olive oil

2 tbsp (30 ml) vegetable stock

1 yellow onion, diced

7 cloves garlic, minced

½ tsp salt, plus more to taste

¼ tsp freshly ground black pepper, plus more to taste

⅛ tsp ground nutmeg

4 cups (120 g) fresh baby spinach, chopped

1 cup (240 ml) heavy whipping cream

4 oz (113 g) softened cream cheese

1 cup (113 g) shredded mozzarella cheese

½ cup (57 g) shredded pepper jack cheese

Add the olive oil, stock, onion, garlic, salt, pepper, nutmeg and spinach to the Instant Pot.

Secure the lid with the vent in the closed position. Press the "Steam" button. Use the "–/+" button until the time display reads 1 minute.

Once the timer sounds, quick release the steam. Press the "Sauté" button.

Add the heavy cream, cream cheese, mozzarella and pepper jack to the pot. Mix to combine and sauté for 2 minutes.

Hit "Cancel" and then cover the pot with the lid. Let the spinach sit, covered, for about 4 minutes.

Remove the lid, mix and add more salt and pepper if needed.

TIP: This is best served the day it's made.

SESAME-HONEY MUSTARD *Shishito* PEPPERS

PREP TIME: 10 MINUTES
COOK TIME: 2 MINUTES
SERVES 4-6

Bet you guys didn't know that you could achieve beautiful charred shishito peppers without the grill, broiler or dangerously holding tongs over an open burner on your stove. These peppers are charred and steamed to tender perfection. I serve them alongside a slightly creamy and spicy Asian honey-mustard sauce to reinforce that kick of heat and then bring it back down a notch.

1 tbsp (12 g) mayonnaise

1 tbsp (12 g) plain, nonfat Greek yogurt

1 tbsp (12 g) Dijon mustard

⅛ tsp horseradish

⅛ tsp chili-garlic sauce

1 tbsp (15 ml) honey

Pinch of salt

1 tsp rice wine vinegar

½ tsp sesame oil

12 oz (340 g) shishito peppers

½ cup (120 ml) water

Sesame seeds, for garnish

Add the mayonnaise, yogurt, mustard, horseradish, chili-garlic sauce, honey, salt and vinegar to a small bowl. Whisk to combine.

Press "Sauté." Add the sesame oil, 1 tablespoon (15 ml) of the yogurt-honey-mustard sauce and the peppers to the pot. Toss with tongs to combine.

Sauté for about 10 minutes, turning and tossing the peppers three or four times only. You want them to char on the outside.

After 10 minutes, remove the peppers. Add the water and steam trivet to the pot. Place a small square of foil on top of the trivet. Add the peppers back to the pot, placing them on top of the foil.

Secure the lid with the steam vent closed. Press "Pressure Cook" until the display light is beneath "Low Pressure." Adjust the "–/+" button until the time display reads 2 minutes.

When the timer sounds, quick release the pressure. Use tongs to transfer the peppers to a serving platter. Garnish with sesame seeds, and serve with sauce on the side for dipping.

SALSA-STYLE REFRIED BLACK BEANS WITH *Bacon*

PREP TIME: 15 MINUTES
COOK TIME: 7 MINUTES
SERVES 4-6

Back when I was a poor college student, I ate canned vegetarian refried beans as a meal on the reg. Before you get all grossed out, know that I added all the things to it. Salsa and hot sauce is a natural choice. Top it with cheese and some salad ingredients, and then—boom!—burrito bowl on the cheap. This is the upscale(ish) version of that, using bacon and my Big-Batch Black Beans (page 160). We aren't poor college students anymore, so why eat like it?

4 slices raw bacon, chopped

½ yellow onion, diced

1 (4.5-oz [127-g]) can diced green chilies

1 clove garlic, grated

1 (14.5-oz [411-g]) can fire-roasted diced tomatoes

3 cups (450 g) Big-Batch Black Beans (page 160) or 2 (14.5-oz [411-g]) cans black beans, drained and rinsed

¼ cup (60 ml) low-sodium chicken stock

½ tsp salt

¼ tsp freshly ground black pepper

Shredded Mexican-blend cheese, for topping, optional

Not-Another-Restaurant Salsa (page 163), for topping, optional

Pico de gallo, for topping, optional

Press "Sauté," and wait 1 to 2 minutes for the Instant Pot to warm up. Add the bacon and cook until crispy. Remove it with a slotted spoon and transfer it to a paper towel–lined plate.

Add the onion and green chilies, and scrape off the burnt bits of bacon from the bottom of the pot. Once the onion starts to become translucent, in 3 to 5 minutes, add the garlic and stir to combine. Press "Cancel."

Mix in the tomatoes, beans, stock, salt and pepper.

Secure the lid with the vent in the closed position. Press "Pressure Cook" until the display light is underneath "High Pressure." Use the "−/+" button to adjust the time until the display reads 7 minutes.

Once the beans are done, quick release the steam.

Remove the lid and carefully stir the bean mixture to combine. Use an immersion blender to puree the beans until smooth.

Reheat the bacon in the microwave for 7 seconds. Top the beans with the bacon, the cheese and salsa or pico de gallo, if using.

CILANTRO-LIME *Quinoa*

PREP TIME: 5 MINUTES
COOK TIME: 1 MINUTES
SERVES 4

A long, long time ago on the blog, I had a recipe go viral. It was for blackened chicken and cilantro-lime quinoa. That was back in 2011. This quinoa is still my go-to side dish for Mexican food or spicy meat dishes. Cooking the quinoa on the stovetop can be tricky, though. If you have the heat too high or overcook the quinoa, just like rice, it can turn gummy or hard and watery. But with the Instant Pot, you can get perfectly cooked quinoa every single time.

1 cup (240 ml) vegetable stock, chicken stock or water

1 cup (180 g) quinoa

¼ tsp salt, plus more to taste

¼ tsp freshly ground black pepper, plus more to taste

Zest of 1 lime

Juice of ½ lime

2 tbsp (2 g) fresh chopped cilantro

Add the stock or water and the quinoa, salt, pepper and lime zest to the Instant Pot. Mix to combine.

Secure the lid and place the vent in the closed position. Press "Pressure Cook" until the light is underneath "High Pressure." Use the "−/+" button until the time displays 1 minute.

When the timer sounds, natural release the pressure for 15 minutes. Quick release the remaining pressure.

Remove the lid and fluff the quinoa with a fork. Mix in the lime juice and cilantro. Adjust the salt and pepper to taste.

BLACK BEAN & MANGO *Brown* RICE

PREP TIME: 10 MINUTES
COOK TIME: 15 MINUTES
SERVES 4-6

I would like you to meet the burrito bowl's new best friend: Black Bean & Mango Brown Rice. It is packed with flavor yet still subtle enough to complement any taco meat or veggie. I love this rice because you seriously just dump everything in your Instant Pot, give it a stir and then—magic! Use canned black beans if you are out of my perfect Big-Batch Black Beans (page 160) or frozen mango if you don't have access to a fresh mango. This rice makes the perfect taco night sidekick.

1¼ cups (300 ml) chicken stock

1 cup (190 g) brown rice

1 cup (150 g) Big-Batch Black Beans (page 160)

¾ cup (125 g) diced mango

1 jalapeño, seeded and diced

½ tsp ground cumin

¼ tsp onion powder

¼ tsp garlic powder

¼ tsp cayenne pepper

½ tsp salt, plus more to taste

¼ tsp freshly ground black pepper, plus more to taste

1 tbsp (1 g) chopped fresh cilantro

1 tsp lime juice

Add the stock, rice, beans, mango, jalapeño, cumin, onion powder, garlic powder, cayenne, salt and pepper to the Instant Pot. Mix to combine.

Secure the lid and move the vent to the closed position. Press "Pressure Cook" until the light is underneath "High Pressure." Use the "–/+" button to change the time display to read 15 minutes.

When the time is up, allow the pressure to natural release for 20 minutes. Once the rice is cooked, quick release any remaining pressure.

Remove the lid and fluff the rice with a fork.

Add more salt and pepper to taste along with the cilantro and lime juice. Mix to combine.

PINTO BEAN *Tinga*

Back when I was working an unbearable office job with one of my best friends, we used to have monthly potluck lunches. The only thing that made that job tolerable, aside from being with my friend every day, was when one of my coworkers would bring in chicken tinga. I would go back for seconds and thirds of that fiery, tomato-coated meat. This is my version of that smoky and spicy sauce. It's good on anything but especially a batch of hearty pinto beans. I like these as a side on taco night or on top of a tostada.

1 (14.5-oz [411-g]) can fire-roasted diced tomatoes

1 tbsp (15 ml) red enchilada sauce

1 canned chipotle pepper

1 tsp Blackening Seasoning Mix (page 168)

1¾ cups (420 ml) water

1¼ cups (335 g) dried pinto beans, rinsed

1 yellow onion, diced

1 tsp salt, plus more to taste

Add the tomatoes, enchilada sauce, chipotle pepper and Blackening Seasoning Mix to a food processor. Puree until smooth.

Pour the sauce, along with the water and beans, into the Instant Pot.

Mix in the onion and salt.

Secure the lid with the vent in the sealed position. Press "Pressure Cook" until the light is underneath "High Pressure." Use the "–/+" button to adjust the time until the display reads 50 minutes.

Once the beans are cooked, allow the pressure to natural release.

Remove the lid, and mix the beans. Add more salt if needed.

COCONUT RICE *Pilaf*

PREP TIME: 10 MINUTES
COOK TIME: 3 MINUTES
SERVES 4-6

My dad spent some time in Hawaii during his stint in the Army. He has since sworn off all pineapple and coconut things. Being the loving daughter I am, I make it my goal to get him to eat these things anyway. Traditional rice pilaf consists of rice and toasted nuts. It's deliciously simple, even when you sneak in some coconut milk, shredded coconut and macadamia nuts. This rice is a dream and steams up so easily. I would highly recommend it to anyone skeptical about coconut. It pairs well with a nice piece of fish or chicken or makes a light lunch.

2 tsp (10 ml) extra-virgin olive oil

1 onion, finely diced

1 clove garlic, grated

1 cup (190 g) long-grain jasmine rice, rinsed

½ tsp coriander

½ tsp ground cumin

¼ tsp freshly ground black pepper

½ tsp salt

1 tsp orange zest

⅓ cup (80 ml) coconut milk

⅔ cup (160 ml) water

½ cup (75 g) chopped macadamia nuts

⅓ cup (30 g) unsweetened shredded coconut flakes

1 tsp fresh chopped basil

1 tsp fresh chopped parsley

Press "Sauté" on the Instant Pot and wait 1 minute for it to heat. Add the olive oil along with the onion, garlic and rice. Cook the rice, stirring regularly, for 3 minutes. Press "Cancel."

Season the rice with the coriander, cumin, pepper, salt and orange zest. Mix to combine.

Mix in the coconut milk and water.

Secure the lid, with the vent in the closed position. Press "Pressure Cook" until the display light is beneath "High Pressure." Use the "−/+" button to adjust the time to read 3 minutes.

While the rice cooks, toast the nuts and coconut in a dry pan over a low flame for 5 minutes. Stir regularly to prevent any burning.

When the Instant Pot's timer goes off, allow the pressure to natural release for 15 minutes. Quick release any remaining pressure.

Remove the lid and fluff the rice with a fork. Transfer it to a serving bowl.

Mix in the toasted coconut and nuts along with the basil and parsley.

Kimchi FRIED RICE

PREP TIME: 10 MINUTES
COOK TIME: 3 MINUTES
SERVES 4-6

When Mike and I used to live in the city, our neighbor, a tiny elderly Korean woman, would spend most weekends outside on her deck making kimchi. At the time, I had no clue what she was doing. If I had, I would have snagged some from her. Kimchi adds so much to any dish, and I always have it with fried rice. It is the perfect way to introduce somebody to kimchi and convert them to a lover of this spicy, fermented stuff. With the Instant Pot, you can switch from rice steamer to rice fryer in a matter of minutes.

1 cup (190 g) jasmine rice

1 cup (240 ml) water

½ cup (75 g) chopped jarred kimchi

½ tsp salt

4 slices raw bacon, chopped

½ yellow onion, diced

½ tsp sriracha

2 tbsp (30 ml) soy sauce

½ cup (75 g) frozen peas

4 green onions, sliced, for garnish

Sesame seeds, for garnish

Rinse the rice in a strainer under cold water.

Add the rice, water, kimchi and salt to the Instant Pot. Mix to combine.

Secure the lid with the steam valve sealed. Press "Pressure Cook" until the light is beneath "High Pressure." Use the "−/+" button to adjust the time until the display reads 3 minutes.

Once the timer sounds, allow the steam to natural release for 10 minutes. Remove the lid and fluff the rice with a fork.

Transfer the rice to a large bowl. Rinse and dry the insert and add it back into the Instant Pot. Press "Sauté" and add the bacon and onion to the Instant Pot. Sauté for 7 minutes, stirring regularly until the bacon is crisp.

Mix in the sriracha and soy sauce, deglazing the bottom of the pot.

Add the rice back to the pot. Stir in the peas. Keep stirring until all the rice is coated in the sauce.

Press "Cancel," and then transfer the rice to a serving dish. Top with the green onions and sesame seeds.

LEMON & GARLIC BUTTER STEAMED *Artichokes*

PREP TIME: 10 MINUTES
COOK TIME: 10 MINUTES
SERVES 4

I learned how to properly eat an artichoke and bite the meat off each leaf during my sophomore year of high school, from a classmate's how-to speech. Who knew there would be such a useful life lesson that day? Perfectly steamed artichokes filled with butter and lemon juice between all the leaves is the perfect appetizer or side. These artichokes are definitely worth the upfront work of trimming the leaves.

4 artichokes

1 cup (240 ml) water

4 tbsp (60 g) butter, room temperature

1 clove garlic, grated

4 lemon slices

Remove the stems from the artichokes. Peel off the bottom, purple-colored leaves. Cut off the top ½ inch (1.3 cm) of the artichokes. Use kitchen shears to trim the pointy top of every leaf.

Pour the water into the Instant Pot. Insert the steam trivet.

Mash together the butter and grated garlic in a small bowl.

Place 1 tablespoon (15 g) of butter on the cut top of each artichoke. Cover the butter with a lemon slice, pressing it down into the butter. Continue until all the artichokes are topped with butter and lemon slices.

Place the artichokes on the steam trivet, lemon side up. Secure the lid with the steam vent sealed. Press "Pressure Cook" until the display light is underneath "High Pressure." Use the "−/+" button to adjust the time until the display reads 10 minutes.

Once the artichokes are done, quick release the steam.

Remove the lid and use tongs to transfer the artichokes to a serving platter.

Remove the lemon slice before eating, squeezing the juice over the leaves.

GREEN BEAN & MUSHROOM *Piccata*

PREP TIME: 8 MINUTES
COOK TIME: 5 MINUTES
SERVES 4

Piccata in Italian apparently means annoyed. I sort of get it. Chicken is good, but chicken that's annoyed or piccata-ed is way better. Same thing with green beans and mushrooms. With a dash of butter and lemon, they are okay. But piccata them and . . . wow! Sauté the mushrooms until they turn crisp and golden, top them with green beans and all that piccata power, then hit the steam setting, and you won't be anywhere near annoyed at the end of the cooking process.

2 tbsp (30 g) unsalted butter

1 tbsp (15 ml) extra-virgin olive oil

4 oz (113 g) cremini mushrooms, stemmed and sliced

2 cloves garlic, grated

¼ cup (60 ml) dry white wine

1 lb (450 g) fresh green beans, trimmed

⅓ cup (80 ml) lemon juice

2 tsp (6 g) drained capers

Salt, to taste

Freshly ground black pepper, to taste

1 tsp fresh chopped parsley, for garnish

Add the butter and olive oil to the Instant Pot. Press the "Sauté" button. Add the mushrooms and sauté for 10 minutes, stirring regularly until the mushrooms turn golden and crisp on the edges. Press the "Cancel" button.

Add the garlic and stir to combine. Pour in the wine and deglaze the bottom of the pot.

Add the green beans, lemon juice, capers, salt and pepper and mix.

Secure the lid with the vent in the sealed position. Press the "Steam" button. Use the "−/+" button until the time display reads 5 minutes.

Once the beans are done, quick release the steam.

Use tongs to remove the beans and mushrooms. Pour the remaining sauce over the beans and mushrooms. Top with more salt and pepper if needed. Garnish with freshly chopped parsley.

Italian WHITE BEANS

PREP TIME: 5 MINUTES
COOK TIME: 50 MINUTES
SERVES 4–6

On any given night of the week, you can find me pulling different sauces and beans from my freezer, trying to make a meal out of what we have. I am very happy with these tomato- and herb-coated Italian white beans on some toast. Serve it over noodles or with an egg and bacon on top if you need something more complex. Even if you run out of your freezer stash, you don't have to wait overnight for the beans to soak to replenish your supply (which is key to my survival and sanity). In an hour, you can have a perfect meal or side dish at the ready.

1¼ cups (230 ml) dry cannellini or great northern beans

2½ cups (600 ml) water

1 (10.75-oz [305-g]) can condensed tomato soup

1 tsp salt, plus more to taste

¼ tsp freshly ground black pepper, plus more to taste

⅛ tsp crushed red pepper flakes

⅛ tsp garlic powder

1 sprig fresh thyme

1 Parmesan rind

1 tbsp (3 g) fresh chopped basil

1 tbsp (5 g) fresh chopped parsley

Combine the beans, water, tomato soup, salt, pepper, red pepper flakes, garlic powder, thyme, Parmesan rind, basil and parsley in the Instant Pot. Mix to coat the beans. Secure the lid with the vent sealed. Press "Pressure Cook" until the light display is beneath "High Pressure," and then use the "–/+" button to adjust the time until the display reads 50 minutes.

When the timer sounds, allow the pressure to natural release. Once the float valve has completely gone down, remove the lid. Stir the beans. Add more salt and pepper to taste. Remove any remnant of the Parmesan rind.

Store the beans in freezer-safe, sealable jars or containers in the refrigerator for up to 1 week or in the freezer for up to 1 month.

BROWN BUTTER, COCOA & CHILI *Acorn Squash*

PREP TIME: 5 MINUTES
COOK TIME: 2 MINUTES
SERVES 4–6

The seasoning combination on this squash is bonkers—totally out of this world. It is almost like an instant mole sauce. Sort of. The squash is steamed perfectly and then crisped up in the brown butter sauce. It will have people who aren't veggie lovers yelling at you for making them like things they normally hate. I speak from experience.

1 medium acorn squash

1 cup (240 ml) water

¼ cup (60 g) unsalted butter

½ tsp salt

½ tsp dark unsweetened cocoa powder

1 tsp chili powder

Prepare the acorn squash by slicing it down the middle from top to bottom. Use a spoon to scoop out all the seeds and fibrous strands from the center. Place each half cut side down, and then slice them into ⅓-inch (7-mm) half-moon slices.

Insert the steam trivet into the Instant Pot. Pour the water down into the pot. Arrange the squash on top of the trivet.

Secure the lid with the steam vent sealed. Press "Pressure Cook" until the light is beneath "High Pressure." Use the "–/+" button to adjust the time until the display reads 2 minutes.

Once the squash is steamed, quick release the pressure. Remove the lid and use tongs to transfer the squash to a small baking sheet.

Remove the trivet and dump out the water.

Press "Sauté" and add the butter. Use a rubber spatula to stir the butter until it starts to lightly brown, 5 to 7 minutes.

Whisk in the salt, cocoa and chili powder.

Add the squash slices back into the pot and sauté for about 2 minutes on each side. Work in batches until all the slices have been coated in the sauce and are slightly crisped up on the edges.

Press "Cancel." Transfer the cooked slices to a serving platter. Pour the remainder of the sauce on top of the squash.

NEXT-LEVEL STAPLES

Not to pat myself on the back, but the recipes in this book are all pretty stellar. They aren't what you would normally think can be made in your Instant Pot. I am really proud of that fact. Most of the recipes call for the addition of one of my staples because, like the title says, they bring the dish to the next level.

Blackening Seasoning Mix (page 168) and Spicy Zhoug Sauce (page 164) can be added to any dish for a little extra depth and spice. Not only are the Just-Right Jammy Eggs (page 159) my breakfast pretty much every day of my life, they are a great topping for the "Gimme-All-the-Mushrooms" Ramen (page 76), Mixed Vegetable Lo Mein (page 87) and Tex-Mex Chorizo Chilaquiles (page 20).

Make the Big-Batch Black Beans (page 160) and Not-Another-Restaurant Salsa (page 163), and then serve them alongside the gazillions of Mexican recipes in this book. Save yourself money and get restaurant-quality meals in your own home.

I could have included the Perfect Shredded Chicken (Hold the Chicken Stock) (page 156) in the meat and main dish chapter, but I make it so often, it has become a staple. A staple to me is something you always turn to when you are either low on inspiration or ingredients. Stocking your freezer, fridge and pantry with these bad boys will set you up for cooking success any day of the week.

Perfect SHREDDED CHICKEN (HOLD THE CHICKEN STOCK)

PREP TIME: 5 MINUTES
COOK TIME: 15 MINUTES
YIELDS ABOUT 3 CUPS (420 G)

My pet peeve with shredded chicken is all that liquid! I don't want to make chicken stock every single time I need some shredded chicken for soup, chili or tacos. Am I right? This recipe does yield a little liquid but not enough to annoy you or to require storage and freezing. The chicken still stays juicy, fear not. You can add any seasoning you like and cater the chicken to whatever you're eating that day. I'd say that's pretty perfect!

3 large boneless, skinless chicken breasts

1 tbsp (15 ml) water

Salt and pepper, to taste

Add the chicken to the pressure cooker along with the water.

Secure the lid with the vent sealed. Press the "Pressure Cook" button. Press the "Pressure Level" button until "High" is selected. Hit the "-/+" button to adjust the time until the display reads 15 minutes.

After 15 minutes, natural release the pressure for 7 minutes. Quick release any remaining pressure. Add desired seasonings along with salt and pepper.

Shred the chicken using two forks. Mix to distribute the seasoning.

JUST-RIGHT JAMMY *Eggs*

My mom follows me on social media. It's awesome but also has downsides. Every morning I eat an egg and post a picture on social media—because if you don't post it, did it really happen? But now that my mom sees it, she makes classic mom comments such as "If I have to see another picture of an egg, I'm going to go crazy." So I stopped posting and put the egg in the book. Take that, Mom! Cooking eggs in the Instant Pot is my new go-to method. You don't have to worry about setting a timer to ensure the egg is properly cooked. You also don't run the risk of forgetting about the boiling pot of water and almost burning down your house. Not that I am speaking from personal experience. On the plus side, you get perfect eggs every single time.

1 cup (240 ml) water

6–12 large eggs

Insert the steam rack into the Instant Pot. Add the water. Place the eggs on top of the steam rack.

Secure the lid and close the pressure valve. Press the "Steam" button. Press the "–/+" button until the display reads 5 minutes. Make sure the "Keep Warm" button is not lit, as this will overcook the eggs.

Fill a small bowl with ice cubes and water. Once the eggs are done steaming, carefully quick release the pressure valve. Use tongs to transfer the eggs to the ice bath.

Peel the eggs and eat them immediately, or place them in the refrigerator for up to 1 week.

BIG-BATCH *Black Beans*

PREP TIME: 10 MINUTES
COOK TIME: 25 MINUTES
SERVES 4–6

I have never said to myself, that meal prep was a waste of time. Especially when that prep doesn't involve soaking beans overnight. In our house, Big-Batch Black Beans go into containers and straight to the freezer. Portion out one-and-a-half cups into each container, and add one portion to some chili and another to a rice dish and use another as a taco topping. Whenever you can save yourself time or a trip to the store, do it!

1 lb (450 g) dry black beans

6 cups (1.4 L) water or low-sodium chicken stock

2 cloves garlic, peeled and smashed

1 dried bay leaf

1 tsp ground cumin

Pinch of crushed red pepper flakes

2 tsp (8 g) salt

1 onion, halved

Sort through the beans and pick out any that are cracked or discolored.

Add the beans, water or stock, garlic, bay leaf, cumin, red pepper flakes, salt and onion halves to the Instant Pot. Mix to combine.

Secure the lid with the steam vent sealed. Press "Pressure Cook" and make sure the light is beneath "High Pressure." Use the "–/+" button to adjust the time until the display reads 25 minutes.

When the beans are done, allow the pressure to manually release for 10 minutes. Quick release any residual pressure.

Remove the lid. Discard the bay leaf and onion halves. Stir to combine.

Transfer the beans to heat-proof and freezer-safe containers with lids. Store them in the refrigerator for up to 1 week or in the freezer for up to 6 months.

NOT-ANOTHER-RESTAURANT *Salsa*

My friend taught me the secret to making restaurant-quality salsa at home—canned fire-roasted tomatoes—and I have never again bought a jar of salsa. With this quick and easy recipe, you'll be able to whip up restaurant-quality salsa at home any time you please. This can be added to my Perfect Shredded Chicken (Hold the Chicken Stock) (page 156) for tacos, used to top off any chili or to spice up a Just-Right Jammy Egg (page 159). I still prefer the chip-to-mouth delivery method though.

2 cloves garlic

½ cup (8 g) fresh cilantro

¼ cup (40 g) chopped yellow onion

1 jalapeño, seeded and chopped

1 (14.5-oz [411-g]) can fire-roasted diced tomatoes

½ tsp salt, plus more to taste

¼ tsp freshly ground black pepper, plus more to taste

½ tsp ground cumin

Big pinch of crushed red pepper flakes

Juice of 1 lime

Add the garlic, cilantro, onion and jalapeño to the bowl of a food processor. Pulse until finely chopped.

Add the tomatoes, salt, pepper, cumin, red pepper flakes and lime juice to the food processor. Puree until mostly smooth or to the consistency you desire.

Add more salt and pepper to taste.

Feel free to add a canned chipotle pepper, a 4.5-ounce (127-g) can of green chilies or even ¼ cup (40 g) of mango to this recipe to jazz it up.

Spicy ZHOUG SAUCE

Ever need a little extra kick to your food? Forget hot sauce—this is going to be your new topping of choice. It is a spicy Middle Eastern sauce similar to chimichurri. Put a little on top of scrambled eggs, mix it in with shredded chicken for tacos, or even whisk it together with your favorite salad dressing. This sauce is always in the back of my fridge because we are a family who likes a little heat.

2 cloves garlic, roughly chopped

1 jalapeño, half the seeds removed, roughly chopped

1½ cups (24 g) fresh cilantro

1½ cups (90 g) fresh parsley

¼ tsp crushed red pepper flakes

½ tsp salt, plus more to taste

¼ tsp freshly ground black pepper, plus more to taste

1 tsp ground cumin

1 tsp coriander

½ cup (120 ml) olive oil

1½ tsp (8 ml) red wine vinegar

Add the garlic, jalapeño, cilantro, parsley and red pepper flakes to a food processor. Pulse until finely chopped.

Add the salt, pepper, cumin, coriander, olive oil and red wine vinegar to the food processor. Puree until the zhoug sauce is combined and just about smooth.

Add more salt and pepper to taste.

TOMATO-GARLIC *Sauce*

PREP TIME: 10 MINUTES
COOK TIME: 30 MINUTES
YIELDS 2½ CUPS (600 ML)

When I was younger, I used to eat tomatoes like apples—seeds and all. I usually hoard all the tomatoes from my parents' garden in the summer and eat cherry tomatoes as snacks. Whatever tomatoes I don't eat are used to make big batches of tomato sauce to freeze for wintertime. There is one hiccup in this plan: Nobody wants to have the stove and oven on for a long period of time in the middle of summer. Enter your old friend the Instant Pot. You can now get that deep roasted-tomato flavor without the hot house in 30 minutes.

2 pints (300 g) grape tomatoes, halved

4 cloves garlic, smashed

½ cup (75 g) diced onion

1 tsp salt, plus more to taste

½ tsp freshly ground black pepper, plus more to taste

½ cup (120 ml) olive oil

¼ cup (60 ml) red wine

2 tbsp (32 g) tomato paste

Add the tomatoes, garlic, onion, salt, pepper, oil, red wine and tomato paste to the Instant Pot. Mix until the tomato paste is incorporated.

Secure the lid with the steam valve closed. Press the "Pressure Cook" button. Adjust the pressure to "High Pressure." Press the "−/+" button until the display reads 30 minutes.

Once the tomatoes are done cooking, quick release the steam.

Remove the lid. Use an immersion blender to puree the sauce until smooth or transfer it to a blender when it's slightly cooled and puree it until smooth.

Add more salt and pepper to taste.

Transfer the sauce to an airtight container with a lid and store it in the refrigerator for up to 10 days or freeze it for up to 3 months.

BLACKENING SEASONING *Mix*

PREP TIME: 5 MINUTES
YIELDS ½ CUP (58 G)

One of my all-time, most popular recipes on the blog is my blackened chicken. It is full of flavor and has zero frills. You should already have most of these spices in your pantry. Add some of this seasoning mix to any meat or bean recipe in this book for an extra kick. Mix it up and keep it in your pantry for a day when you need a little dinner inspiration.

1 tbsp (7 g) smoked paprika

½ tsp cayenne pepper

½ tsp garlic powder

½ tsp ground cumin

½ tsp onion powder

¼ tsp crushed red pepper flakes

½ tsp salt

¼ tsp freshly ground black pepper

Whisk together all the spices in a small mixing bowl. Transfer the mix to a sealable container. The seasoning will keep for 1 month.

ACKNOWLEDGMENTS

Back when I got the first email about making a cookbook, I seriously thought it was spam. Thankfully, I took the chance and replied just in case it was for real. Thank you to all my family and friends who took me seriously when I started my food blog and the endeavor of writing this book.

Thank you to all my kid watchers, food tasters, food critiquers and behind-the-scene cheerleaders. You guys all know who you are, and I love you! Thank you to all my visible and invisible Internet friends who keep reading Sarcastic Cooking. You guys really make a girl feel special.

Thank you to Caitlin at Page Street Publishing for liking my writing voice and making sure it had a chance to be heard in this book. Thank you to Will and the entire Page Street team for walking me through the trials and tribulations involved with this book's creation.

Thank you to Ariana and the entire Jean V. Naggar Literary Agency, Inc. for listening to my rants and reading many, many emails. Thank you for talking me off the ledge more than once and making me feel less crazy.

Special thanks to Crock-Pot and Calphalon for outfitting me with amazing pots, pans and cooking devices. Thank you Typhoon Housewares and Cookware for the beautiful bowls and platters featured in this book. All these images wouldn't look as pretty without Erickson Surfaces as backgrounds.

I want to give a shout-out to all my girl boss bloggers I am lucky enough to call my tribe. Thank you all for inspiring me to do more and to not be afraid of the unknown. Thank you for always answering my questions or telling me to just get up and do it!

Last, and most important, thank you for buying this book. Thank you for putting your faith in me to help you make food to nourish yourself, friends or family.

ABOUT THE AUTHOR

STEFANIE BUNDALO is the founder of the popular food blog Sarcastic Cooking. Her work has been featured in *Better Homes & Gardens*, Buzzfeed, *The Huffington Post* and Shape.com. Prior to starting the blog in 2011, Stefanie worked as a restaurant inspector, catering manager and every job in between. She and her family live in a suburb outside of Chicago, where she is a stay-at-home/work-at-home mom to two young boys and an elderly pug. She is married to her college sweetheart, who also acts as her head taste tester and blog editor. She is a craft beer, food and multi-cooker enthusiast. Stefanie believes cooking shouldn't have to take a long time or be complicated to be delicious. Food is fun, so why take it too seriously?

INDEX